IMAGES
of America

TAMPA BAY
HOTEL

Improvements in rail and steamship travel during the 19th century resulted in Florida's rise as a popular tourist destination between 1890 and 1930. While Americans used their disposable income to travel, they developed a fascination with collecting souvenirs. A variety of Florida keepsakes featured the Tampa Bay Hotel. Mementos included match holders, cups, china plates, spoons, forks, puzzles, wooden trinket boxes, metal banks, crumb trays, paperweights, match strikers, fruit bowls, letter openers, playing cards, calendars, pencils, and a hand-carved conch shell. (Henry B. Plant Museum.)

ON THE COVER: The Tampa Bay Hotel, situated on the west bank of the Hillsborough River, was an impressive structure for visitors to gaze upon as their train pulled into Tampa. During its 41 years of operation (1891–1932), the hotel was a sports destination, tranquil oasis, social center, and international wonder. (Henry B. Plant Museum archives.)

IMAGES
of America

TAMPA BAY
HOTEL

Enjoy exploring the Tampa Bay Hotel.

Heather T. Brown
Susan V. Carter

Heather Trubee Brown and Susan V. Carter
Foreword by Cynthia Gandee Zinober
Introduction by Charles McGraw Groh

ARCADIA
PUBLISHING

Published by Arcadia Publishing
Charleston, South Carolina

Printed in the United States of America

Library of Congress Control Number: 2019944899

For all general information, please contact Arcadia Publishing:
Telephone 843-853-2070
Fax 843-853-0044
E-mail sales@arcadiapublishing.com
For customer service and orders:
Toll-Free 1-888-313-2665

Visit us on the Internet at www.arcadiapublishing.com

For my husband, Racine, and children, Rolton and Ella—thank you for your limitless patience and support, willingness to read Mommy's work, and hugs. —HTB

To John, Johnathan, Caroline, and Bandit for giving me the time to compile this book, and to my mother, Mary Ann Woodruff, and late father, Frank Vasiloff, who ignited my love of history and the past. —SVC

CONTENTS

FOREWORD

The professional staff of the Henry B. Plant Museum is delighted to share the fascinating stories of the Tampa Bay Hotel, one of the most imaginative creations of America's Gilded Age. Since 1891, the building has been the architectural icon for the city of Tampa.

For over 40 years, wealthy guests stayed and played at the hotel, often after arriving in private railcars. We hope this book will transport you to the age of early Florida tourism. The era was anything but sedentary. Frivolity, romance, and excitement permeated daily life at the hotel, and this is the tone we have used to bring history to life in this book. Theater, musical performances, fine dining, dancing, garden parties, boating, fishing, tennis competitions, and hunting were just some of the activities that made up the daily calendar of things to do at the Tampa Bay Hotel.

Bringing the hotel's story to life has always involved people of enormous diversity; those who visited, who worked here, who performed here, and who made it possible. We all love learning about other people, meeting people, making connections, and hearing stories. We hope you will be charmed by the lifestyle details in this book. For many decades, the museum has given great importance to the collection of rare hotel images, and we are delighted to give you our favorites in the following pages.

It was Henry Plant's vision that brought this incredible resort to the people, and it was his vision that made the Plant System of hotels, railroads, and steamships a success. He did more for the City of Tampa than anyone else who has been here since.

—Cynthia Gandee Zinober
Executive Director
Henry B. Plant Museum

ACKNOWLEDGMENTS

The majority of images in this publication are from the Henry B. Plant Museum archives. Many donors have contributed to this outstanding collection including Shirley Evans Besch, Jan and Robin C. Brown, John Browning, Helen A. Davis, Sean Donnelly, Ron Fox, the estate of Lyn Friedt, Paula Gemelli, Robin Robson Gonzalez, Marcia Hansen, Pam Helig, Lyn Hergenrader, John Herrmann, Joyce D. Howell, Inez and Lon Hubbard, George N. Johnson Jr., Joan M. Jones, Elizabeth B. Kelp, Elaine King, Colleen and Rudolf Kratzer, Anna F. Labadie, John T. Lesley, the University of Tampa Macdonald-Kelce Library, Connie Kearns Meadows and the Ferris/Floyd family, Joyce Payne, Jacqueline O'Connor, Alfred N. Page, Helen Ramsdale, W. Steve Rinaldi Sr., Daniel Chase Robinson, Audrey M. Shine, Sylvia Vega Smith, Laura Tallarico, Michael Turbeville, Nancy E. Villarroel, Jane and Jerry Williams, Mary Virginia Wilson, and Cynthia Gandee Zinober. Some of the objects and architecture seen in these photographs have been conserved through the efforts of the Henry B. Plant Museum Society Inc. and the Chiselers Inc., respectively.

We are grateful to the following institutions and sources for giving us permission to include their images. They are identified with the following key:

AMC	American Red Cross
DCDAR	DeSoto Chapter, National Society Daughters of the American Revolution
HD	Hampton Dunn
JFH	J. Fraser Himes
LOC	Library of Congress
MKL	Macdonald-Kelce Library, the University of Tampa
NA	National Archives
RC	Department of College Archives and Special Collections, Olin Library, Rollins College, Winter Park, Florida
RRG	Robin Robson Gonzalez
SAF	State Archives of Florida Memory Project
SFHS	Southwest Florida Historical Society Inc.
THCPLS	Tampa–Hillsborough County Public Library System
TRC	Theodore Roosevelt Collection, Houghton Library, Harvard University

This publication would not have been possible without the support of the Henry B. Plant Museum Board of Trustees and executive director Cynthia Gandee Zinober; the professional staff of Nora Armstrong for digitization and photography, Todd Edwards, Jose Gelats, Lindsay Huban, and Scott Simpson; and interns Emma Bernstine and Shae Donaldson. We appreciate the contributions and expertise of Delphin Acosta, Art Bagley, the City of Tampa, Marlyn Cook, Jennifer Dietz, curatorial volunteer Mona Gardner for fact-checking and editing, Charles McGraw Groh, Robin Nigh, and the University of Tampa.

INTRODUCTION

History has proven a prediction made by *New York Times* reporter William Drysdale in 1892. Recognizing the Tampa Bay Hotel as "one of the great buildings of the world," he prophesied that the ornate structure, "made of brick and iron, glass and mahogany," would be "a building to stand for centuries." This permanence can be credited to architect J.A. Wood, who designed the Tampa Bay Hotel to withstand the fires and hurricanes that claimed so many of the seasonal resorts that once dotted the eastern seaboard. Today, the result of his labors survives as a monument to Gilded Age excess. The immense scale of the building confounds easy description. Indeed, Drysdale confessed his inability to depict the hotel in its entirety; instead, he relied on a list of component parts: "It is built of red brick, with stone and terra cotta trimmings, and its general shape is somewhat crescentic . . . with a dozen silvered domes and minarets rising from its roof." Once inside, he marveled at the immense two-story rotunda—stuffed with bronze statues, fine paintings, carpeting, and armchairs—that greeted arriving guests, as well as the 500-foot hallway that led to the hotel's opulent dining room. The overall effect was dazzling and exotic.

Only decades prior to the Tampa Bay Hotel's opening in 1891, few would have associated the South with tourism and leisure, let alone luxury. Nineteenth-century Americans viewed Florida and the surrounding states as unbearably hot and riddled with disease, a perception reinforced by periodic yellow fever epidemics. Sectional animosities and impassable terrain compounded this negative impression. Perceptions gradually shifted as physicians extolled the healing powers of the region's winter climate and natural mineral springs. The creation of Florida as the premier winter travel destination depended upon the transportation revolution and the ability of railroad magnates Henry Flagler and Henry Plant to meet the demands of the new industrial elite, who craved fashionable consumption, novelty, and entertainment. In 1888, Flagler inaugurated the age of Florida luxury tourism with the opening of the Hotel Ponce de Leon in St. Augustine, and later expanded this resort experience down his railroad line to Palm Beach. Meanwhile, Plant completed the extension of railroad service to the state's west coast. Not to be outdone by his rival, Plant brought architect J.A. Wood to Tampa to erect the magnificent hotel that newspapers across the country quickly dubbed "Plant's Palace."

The Tampa Bay Hotel's ornate turrets, domes, and horseshoe arches highlight a central distinction between winter and summer tourism. Visitors embraced the Florida climate, but the flat and desolate landscape offered little to rival European vistas or northern coasts and mountains. In response, the architects of Florida's grand hotels deviated from the blueprints of summer resorts like the Manhattan Beach Hotel, which used rustic design elements to blend the structure into its picturesque natural surroundings. Florida hotels fabricated their environments. In St. Augustine, the Hotel Ponce de Leon was constructed as a Spanish Renaissance palace, inviting the wealthy into a historical fantasy that capitalized on the city's colonial origins. Plant's grand hotel, erected in close proximity to the unpainted wooden houses, mule carts, and the few humble stores that comprised Tampa, went even further in crafting an exotic illusion; the design relied on Moorish and Islamic elements to fashion the exterior facade into an imaginary oasis that was completely divorced from time and place. Once visitors stepped inside, the hotel's amenities and entertainments rendered the location even more irrelevant. With enough objets d'art to rival a European museum, a casino offering performances by world-famous artists, an orchestra, and a golf course, guests had no reason to interact with the local community.

Tampa experienced profound changes in the years following the arrival of Plant and his grand hotel, many of which are discernible in the city's selection as the point of embarkation for US troops during the Spanish-American War of 1898. By extending the Kissimmee-Orlando line to connect Port Tampa by rail to Jacksonville in the 1880s, Plant transformed the sleepy village into a center of international commerce, as steamships carrying cargo to and from the Caribbean were now linked through Tampa's deep-water port and railroad terminus to manufacturing centers throughout the United States. Capitalizing on these connections, Vincente Martínez Ybor relocated his cigar manufacturing from Key West to Tampa in 1885, and the migration of Cuban cigar workers and their families contributed to the city's rapid rise in population. According to the appeals made by Mayor Myron Gillette and Henry Plant to the secretary of war, these developments made Tampa the ideal headquarters for US Army operations after the United States decided to intervene in the Cuban War of Independence in April 1898. Tampa possessed the closest port to Cuba, and the city's large Cuban population would support US military efforts provided that the conflict resulted in the island's independence rather than American annexation. The argument succeeded, and thousands of troops descended on Tampa. Military leaders, prominent correspondents such as George Kennan and Richard Harding Davis, and American Red Cross nurses occupied every room in the Tampa Bay Hotel and Plant's smaller Inn at Port Tampa. While the hotels basked in the national spotlight, not all news emanating from Tampa was positive. The single railroad line could not keep up with military demands, and trainloads of supplies were backed up as far as Columbia, South Carolina. Soldiers awaiting transport to Cuba suffered from heat, boredom, and disease, especially dysentery. For the city, though, the military mobilization poured $3 million into local enterprises, accelerating Tampa's business expansion.

In subsequent decades, the Tampa Bay Hotel became increasingly identified with the city's new commercial identity. The death of Henry Plant in 1899 initiated a protracted struggle over the proprietorship of the resort's buildings and grounds, culminating in the city's decision in 1904 to purchase the property. That same year witnessed the beginning of two local traditions that became linked to the hotel, both designed to advance business interests. Tampa boosters combined elements of Mardi Gras celebrations with local pirate lore to refashion the city's May Day observance into an elaborate costumed parade; the associated events, which included speeches by the mayor and the board of trade president, culminated in the first Gasparilla Ball, held in the Tampa Bay Hotel dining room. The hotel grounds also became home to the Florida State Fair, featuring exhibits that cast a spotlight on achievements in agriculture and industry. As wealthy tourists increasingly bypassed Tampa in favor of Palm Beach, the hotel reoriented itself to attract business travelers and to profit from the expansion of middle-class automobile tourism.

Like so many of the country's luxury resorts, the Tampa Bay Hotel could not withstand the Great Depression, and its doors closed in 1932. A year later, the city leased the building to the University of Tampa, reserving one wing for a museum. The structure's historical importance, including its role in the staging of the Spanish-American War, led to its recognition as a National Historic Landmark in 1976, further reinforcing predictions that the majestic building will persist for centuries.

—Charles McGraw Groh, PhD
Associate Professor of History
University of Tampa

Marketing materials for the hotel were designed to spark the imagination and inspire a desire to travel to Florida. Effective advertising layouts interspersed the visual impact of the hotel's architecture with highlighted amenities to evoke a sense of the exotic, the romantic, the elegant, the opulent—only for the most discriminating of guests.

One

EXOTIC ARCHITECTURE
OF A GRAND HOTEL

Tampa's landscape in the 1880s was rough and rural. Clapboard houses accommodating a population of fewer than 700 people accented the sandy paths that served as streets. Beyond the town, an endless view of untamed wilderness was undisturbed, except for the flow of the Hillsborough River. When Henry Plant brought the railroad to Tampa in 1884, the shimmering steel of the Plant System's railroads cut a path through the state, creating the skeleton around which central Florida began to grow. In 1886, Plant purchased a stretch of land along the west bank of the Hillsborough River from an orange grower named Jesse Hayden. Plant had a vision. He broke ground for a magnificent hotel in 1888. When he hosted the grand opening of the Tampa Bay Hotel in February 1891, his winter resort and tropical playground encompassed 150 acres and would change the landscape of Tampa forever.

With his rail lines and the development of Port Tampa as a deep-water, international port, tourists arrived in Florida with speed and ease via land or sea. The Tampa Bay Hotel was the most exotic and luxurious accommodation on Florida's west coast. The hotel and grounds were dedicated to leisure. The opulent 511-room resort boasted all the modern amenities, along with spectacular architecture to rival any structure in Europe or the Near East. The Tampa Bay Hotel was poised to be the destination of the century.

Today, the building continues to attract thousands of visitors each year. Architectural historian William Seale states that "architecturally the Tampa Bay Hotel is one of the most fanciful creations of America's Gilded Age." It is a "building conceived in optimism and whimsey that has survived more than a century to become the premier architectural symbol of the city." The former Tampa Bay Hotel survives as one of the last large-scale examples of a Moorish Revival style building in Florida and the nation. The structure is more than a testament to architectural ingenuity. It is the culmination of Plant's overarching vision for the development of Tampa and the west coast of Florida.

Henry Bradley Plant was born in Branford, Connecticut, on October 27, 1819. As a young man, he gained experience in the express shipping business that became the foundation for a very successful future. As a man of vision, Plant built a transportation empire of steamships, steamboats, and railroads that operated over 5,000 miles. He was one of the first individuals to make a significant, lasting, and positive impact on the development of Florida.

Plant's initial land purchase was followed by a second purchase a few years later from Nattie McKay, resulting in a total of 150 acres on which to build the Tampa Bay Hotel. The local newspaper reported that a public holiday was declared in Tampa for the occasion of the hotel's ground breaking in the summer of 1888. (JFH.)

During a site visit to the grounds of the future Tampa Bay Hotel around 1890, Henry Plant (center) is with hotel architect J.A. Wood (second from left in a light suit). They are accompanied by H.C. Cooper, editor of the *Tampa Tribune*; Herman Glogowski, mayor of Tampa; Wilber McCoy, auditor for the South Florida Railroad; Levi P. Morton, vice president of the United States (to the right of Plant); M.J. O'Brien, president of Southern Express Company; S. Sparkman, attorney; W.C. Stevens; Abe Maas; Francis de Chantal Sullivan, private secretary to Plant; B.R. Swoope, superintendent of the South Florida Railroad; and A.C. Wioepple, attorney. This is the only known picture of architect Wood. (DCDAR.)

Prior to 1888, a ferry was the only means to cross the Hillsborough River. With the expectation of future development on the west side of the river, Plant agreed to build the hotel if the Tampa Board of Trade built a bridge spanning the waterway. This 1889 photograph by prominent photographer J.C. Field shows the original Lafayette Street (today Kennedy Boulevard) swing bridge and the hotel under construction.

13

The cornerstone for the hotel was laid on July 26, 1888, with great fanfare. Tampa mayor Herman Glowgowski and other notable public officials attended the event. This early photograph, dated March 1889, shows the scaffolding around the minarets under construction at the north end of the building. Skilled craftsmen included carpenters, plasterers, electricians, plumbers, bricklayers, and construction workers from across the country who traveled to Tampa to work on this project.

Plant selected New York architect J.A. Wood for the hotel project. Between 1866 and 1908, Wood's prolific career produced 40 major works including churches, private residences, hotels, almshouses, armories, and courthouses throughout New York, Pennsylvania, South Carolina, Georgia, Florida, Louisiana, and Cuba. (SAF.)

Construction workers pose before the east front of the hotel around 1891. Detailed notes about the building of the hotel come from the memoir of Alex Browning, Wood's assistant. He wrote that Wood treated the workers fairly and expected a fair day's work: "Mr. Wood kept a supply of medicine for workers . . . and brought oatmeal for the water boys to put a dipper full in each bucketful of water. This kept the men strong and healthy, and . . . was the reason there was so little sickness on the job."

More than 500 people were employed for the construction of the hotel. These workers pose before the Tampa Bay Hotel Company building, the main construction office, around 1890. Built in 1850, the structure was originally a one-room schoolhouse for some of the children in the area. The white clapboard building still stands on the grounds and is managed by the DeSoto Chapter, National Society of the Daughters of the American Revolution. (SAF.)

This photograph by J.C. Field shows the hotel before Plant amended the architectural plans to add the solarium and dining room at the north end of the building, creating a sprawling hotel of approximately 295,000 square feet. This view highlights the prevalence of the horseshoe arch motif in all 735 windows. The thematic continuity is maintained in the interior spaces as the arches are also present in the corridors.

The original swing bridge, with a designated pedestrian path on both sides, opened on November 28, 1888. Today, it is a drawbridge. This civic improvement is one of Plant's lasting legacies. The power plant that he built, identified by its 140-foot-tall smokestack, provided electricity for the hotel.

The Tampa Bay Hotel is unique in design and geographical position. J.A. Wood drew his inspiration for the design from the Alhambra Palace in Granada, Spain, including his use of domes, minarets, horseshoe arches, and geometric patterns. The location of the building offered guests multiple scenic points of entry to the grounds. Arrival was possible via train on the west front, by Lafayette Street at the south gates, or from the Hillsborough River on the east side.

On August 1, 1889, the *Tampa Journal* recorded Wood's comment on the quantity of construction materials. He remarked that 7,576 barrels of shell, 452 train carloads of brick, 2,949 barrels of cement, 69.5 tons of iron, 282 boxes of tin, 242 kegs of nails, 689,000 feet of lumber, and 30 polished granite columns had been used at that time. Metal tanks installed on the roof supplied water to the building. Two of the four tanks can be seen here between the minarets. (THCPLS.)

This c. 1910 view of the roof provides a bird's-eye view of three minarets, two cupolas, and the largest of the three domes. Each tower was crowned with a gold crescent moon, a decorative element inspired by the Moorish Revival architectural style seen in North Africa and parts of Spain and Portugal. Dotting the roof are the chimneys for the guestrooms' fireplaces.

The largest dome sits atop the dining room. Twelve windows encircle the dome and illuminate the surrounding gallery, casting natural light onto the guests' tables below. Chrysanthemum-shaped finials adorn the top of each horseshoe-shaped dormer.

This c. 1893 photograph shows the south entrance to the hotel, denoted by the massive wrought iron gates bearing the "TBH" monogram. Pedestrians, carriages, and later automobiles arriving from Lafayette Street used this entrance to the grounds. The gatehouse, the small structure to the left with decorative metal roof cresting, was the hotel night watchman's office.

New York Times reporter William Drysdale wrote that the original entrance gate in 1891 was "formed from long palmetto trunks driven into the ground and rustic gates." Tall sabal palms stood on either side. In 1893, the original rustic gate was replaced with distinctive ironwork. J.D. Givens photographed this group of tourists standing before the gates during the winter season of 1897–1898.

Advertisements reveal details about the period in which they were printed. *Everybody's Magazine* published this 1905 ad featuring the hotel's architecture, grounds, management, and automobile rides. The Plant System used this image in many promotional items to convey the charm and grandeur of the hotel and the lifestyle it represented.

Guests escaping the chill of winter arrived by train, as pictured here in 1893. Plant built a rail spur off the main line to reach the hotel entrance, so passengers arriving at the hotel merely stepped off their railcar and entered the building with a few short steps. Additional spurs ran along this line to accommodate the private Pullman cars used by some of the wealthier guests.

The symmetry and geometry of the design are characteristics of the 19th-century Moorish Revival style and contribute to the building's imposing aesthetic. The identical domed grand salon (left) and music room (right) flank the west entrance, the main entrance for guests arriving by train. Decorative scrollwork accents the horseshoe arches of the veranda. Lush plantings lined the avenue approaching the hotel, which opened up to reveal this striking entrance.

This 1892 O. Pierre Havens photograph of the west veranda was taken from the edge of the grand salon looking toward the main entrance. A group of people are seated on the veranda facing the music room, perhaps listening to a morning concert, a regular entertainment for guests.

This glass-plate negative view produced by J. Henry Leonhard of Paterson, New Jersey, is dated February 1899. It shows common architectural elements in Wood's designs, including towers, cupolas, domes, verandas, horseshoe arches, and gingerbread woodwork. Features unique to the Tampa Bay Hotel are the minarets and the chrysanthemum window above the main entrance. The plantings by the veranda helped shade the building from the afternoon sun and created a spacious park-like setting for guests to enjoy.

The hotel was designed with a concrete foundation, brick partitions, and reinforced concrete floors, an early example of fireproof construction in Florida. This was a safety feature worth marketing, as fire was a real threat to wooden hotels. Alex Browning explained that steel beams were placed at regular intervals, and the spaces were filled in with concrete. The aggregate of the concrete was broken bricks, oyster shell, white sand, and Rosendale cement, which was reinforced with one-inch T-irons and recycled cable from the Brooklyn Bridge.

This view of the west front, looking toward the dining room, is from the bricked walkway that runs parallel to the tracks, a perspective that would have been enjoyed by guests as their train pulled into the hotel. Small platforms line the path, used by passengers to board or disembark from railcars with ease.

This image shows the Plant System's Savannah, Florida & Western line locomotive pulling into the hotel in 1893. The hotel was not the end of the line. Guests could board trains for Port Tampa, where they could embark for trips to Key West, Cuba, or Jamaica aboard a Plant System steamship.

According to Alex Browning, cement, both poured and cast, was used for various structural elements such as the main stairs leading to the veranda, the window sills, keystones, and skewbacks. Portland cement, imported from Germany or Belgium at a cost of $3 a barrel, was used for these exposed decorative elements because it was lighter in color than natural cement. All the cast stone was made on-site in molds built by a single carpenter.

The length of the veranda was adorned with finely crafted, decorative gingerbread woodwork and horseshoe arches made of cypress wood. Most of the veranda was accented by a single row of this fretwork. An impressive double row denoted the main entrance. Today, only a single row remains.

After the minarets, the horseshoe arches are one of the most prominent features of the building. In the center of both the east and west fronts of the hotel are three airy horseshoe arches formed from terra-cotta brick. Underneath, double doors of solid mahogany denote the main entrances. The majority of the building's exterior is composed of dark red sand-and-lime brick. A brickfield was established in Campville, Florida, (near Gainesville) specifically for the production of these bricks.

This cabinet card captures the hotel from across the Hillsborough River with banners flying on minarets. It was said the flags flew atop the minarets when Plant was in residence. The hotel was one of the first large buildings in Florida to be fully electrified, to have steam heat throughout, and to feature indoor bathrooms accessible to most guest rooms.

The veranda, an essential outdoor room of any Victorian hotel or grand house, was a transitional space between outdoors and indoors, protected from the elements yet surrounded by fresh air and a few potted plants. In this 1893 image, electric lights extend from the walls to illuminate the veranda after dark. Today, these original fixtures still light the veranda using replica Edison carbon filament bulbs to recreate the authentic atmosphere of the Tampa Bay Hotel.

This c. 1892 O. Pierre Havens photograph captures the grandeur of the sweeping 375-foot long, 18-foot wide east veranda. The original floors of both verandas were made of pine wood. In the late 1930s, the boards on the east veranda were replaced with terrazzo flooring as part of a Works Progress Administration project under Pres. Franklin D. Roosevelt's New Deal.

Veranda Tampa Bay Hotel, Tampa, Fla.

Postcard messages disclose personal insights, both matter-of-fact and humorous, of the Tampa Bay Hotel experience. The handwritten message on the back of this postcard, postmarked February 16, 1908, reads, "This is the place you can leave your hard cash." Tourists flocked to Florida for many reasons, but many came for the healing benefits of the warm climate. This view shows guests on the east veranda on a sunny day.

Scores of wooden rocking chairs lined the grand, two-story verandas so guests could take in the fresh air and Florida's lovely winter weather. They gathered here to engage in polite conversation, observe other guests as they strolled about the grounds, read, or simply daydream.

The Hydriotic Esplanade, designed like a pagoda, is visible along the riverbank in this O. Pierre Havens photograph. Guests viewed the river, aquatic life, and boaters from this unusual structure. When the *Tampa Weekly Tribune* reported on the property inventory in 1905, the Hydriotic Esplanade was among the 27 buildings on the grounds.

This stereoscopic view by the H.C. White Company shows a rare perspective of the exterior from the upper floors in 1907. The minarets stand 10 stories tall. From within a minaret, a guest enjoyed a 360-degree vista of early Tampa. The minarets were originally covered with Taylors Old-Style Pointiminster, "a good sample of American made tin," according to Browning. During a major restoration project in the late 1980s, the minarets were re-sheathed in stainless steel. (LOC.)

Plant gave great thought to every aspect of the hotel's design. These columns are decorated with the crescent moon motif carried over from the finials on the minarets to the tops of the columns. Some are also ingeniously functional as cast iron downspouts that carry water from the roof to the cisterns in the basement.

Three of Wood's surviving buildings are listed in the National Register of Historic Places, including the Tampa Bay Hotel, which was listed in 1972. In 1974, it was designated a National Historic Site on the Florida Bicentennial Trail, and in 1976, it became a National Historic Landmark. This photograph is from about 1900.

Not all marketing materials for the hotel were produced by the Plant System. Postcards were an excellent promotional tool that reached distant audiences and usually carried a positive personal endorsement. This design was produced around 1908 by the S. Langsdorf & Company postcard firm of New York. It is one of a 165-card series of Florida-themed cards. Each featured a unique Florida location encircled by three alligators.

Two

DESIGNING LUXURY

Henry and Margaret Plant spared no expense building and furnishing the Tampa Bay Hotel. Henry was personally involved in the planning and design of the building, while Margaret oversaw every aspect of the interior design; her touch could be seen in each decorative element. In the summer of 1889, the Plants attended the Exposition Universelle in Paris. The international fair brought together the finest craftsmen from around the world, providing the Plants with an extensive and comprehensive selection of decorative arts. They filled 41 train cars with furniture, metal statues, exquisite mirrors, enchanting porcelains, inlaid wooden cabinets, and colorful paintings for the Tampa Bay Hotel. The selective mix of European, Asian, Middle Eastern, and American objets d'art represented Margaret's exquisite taste. The decor reflected comfort and opulence, hallmarks of America's Gilded Age and the lifestyle of wealthy society.

Each of the public spaces on the first floor was designed for a specific function and was furnished to impress: the grand salon as a sitting room, the music room for musical entertainments, the ladies' drawing room for unescorted ladies, and the elevator, solarium, and dining room surrounding guests with a sampling of world travels. The interior decor blended Moorish Revival themes, the Florida landscape, and Victorian culture and mores.

All of the newest modern amenities were installed throughout the hotel. Each room was electrified by direct current generated by the power plant built on the grounds. The telephones, "a mysterious little black instrument on the wall, made of vulcanized rubber," in the words of the *New York Times* of January 24, 1892, were made especially for the hotel and allowed guests to call other rooms and service providers within the hotel, in addition to the port or various businesses in Tampa. Two hydraulic Otis elevators, one passenger and one freight, carried steamer trunks and guests to the rooms on the upper floors. Hot and cold running water was supplied to the indoor bathrooms, a feature so memorable that actress Gloria Swanson later recalled soaking "in a big tub for hours" as a little girl.

Today, many of the hotel's original furnishings and decorative art pieces are preserved by the Henry B. Plant Museum as part of its permanent collection.

Newspaper accounts remarked that the hotel was the most beautiful and luxurious resort in the world. The rotunda, or lobby, was the first space guests entered upon arrival. The lavish surroundings set the tone of an exotic locale with 16 polished granite columns, selected works of art, and rugs woven on Eastern looms. The poufs, or roundabout sofas, were topped with life-size bronze-finished sculptures of literary figures. This view is from around 1891, the year the hotel opened.

This stereo card view of the rotunda is dated 1892. The hotel used steam heat in some areas; the radiators are visible in this image. Fireplaces were used in the guest rooms. According to a promotional leaflet, the main office, bookstand, telegraph, and railway offices were located in this area so guests could stay connected while traveling. Stereo cards, available since the 1860s, were produced using a double set of paper prints mounted side-by-side on cardstock. When viewed through a stereoscope, the images appeared as a single three-dimensional image.

This c. 1893 view of the second floor overlooking the rotunda shows a mezzanine with a gallery of art. Select paintings purchased by the Plants while abroad were on display in the gallery. The elaborately carved railing with horseshoe motifs was removed to create a continuous floor and classrooms for the University of Tampa.

According to hotel advertisements, the rotunda was "arranged with such discriminating taste that one is doubly impressed with its infinite variety and the rare quality of its attractiveness" as captured in this 1893 view. Porcelain spittoons were conveniently placed around the sofa to accommodate gentlemen guests. A life-size statue of Esmeralda and her goat, from Victor Hugo's novel *The Hunchback of Notre Dame*, adorns a European pouf. This statue still graces the same location today.

TAMPA BAY HOTEL.

Guests are hereby notified that the Hotel will not be responsible for Loss of Valuables, Money or Jewelry unless same are deposited in the Office, and receipt taken.

DAVID LAUBER, MANAGER.

During the inaugural 1891–1892 season, the hotel entertained 4,367 guests. When guests arrived at the hotel, they checked in by signing the register at the office in the rotunda. Pictured is the earliest known register in existence; it dates from the November 1905 through March 1906 season. Third from the bottom of the page, guest John Jacob Astor IV from New York City signed in on March 14, 1906. In 1912, he perished in the sinking of the RMS *Titanic*. (MKL.)

The museum's archives contain only four guest registers from the hotel's 41 years of operation. This excerpt from the 1922 hotel guest index shows an entry for Kenesaw Mountain Landis dated March 18–19. Theodore Roosevelt appointed Landis as the first commissioner of baseball. Landis and five future baseball hall-of-famers stayed at the hotel during the 1922–1923 season, including Clark Griffith, Leon Goslin, Stanley "Bucky" Harris, Walter Johnson, and Sam Rice.

Guest registers from the 1920s appear to be general record books of guest names grouped alphabetically, instead of registers in which guests signed in. This excerpt records John Philip Sousa arriving on February 3, 1922, accompanied by his valet. He stayed in room 204. Sousa, the "March King," is most remembered for "The Stars and Stripes Forever." His band performed in the hotel's Tampa Bay Casino on February 3, 1922.

The hotel office was located in the corner of the rotunda near the music room. According to an 1896 *Chicago 400 Society, Clubdom, and Travel*, "Twelve or more suites are equipped with fine pianos and in other rooms they may be ordered if desired, with no more trouble or delay than if an extra rocker was wanted. The order was given in the building and equipping of the Tampa Bay [Hotel] that the best of everything without concern as to the cost was to be secured. And it was."

These original brass room keys have tags bearing the room numbers 254 and 110. The message on the reverse advises, "If carried away, return unsealed by mail. Postage 3 cents." Guest rooms could be rented as single rooms or suites of rooms as determined by the manager. Room 110 is in the museum, and the key pictured operates the night latch, an interior lock for extra security.

This 1893 image shows two remarkable pieces from the main corridor by the rotunda, a sculpture known as *Gnomes from the Black Forest* and the monumental Wedgwood floor vase with swans. The vase was the largest piece ever created by the Wedgwood factory. Today, it is on display in the museum and is one of eight known to exist in the world. The gnomes have been lost to time.

Captured in an 1893 brochure image, a Fairbanks Personal Scale stands in a corner of the rotunda. The company advertised, "There is no more important index to general health than personal weight." Fairbanks was one of the most significant 19th-century scale companies in the United States. Also pictured is a life-sized bronzed statue called *Little Red Riding Hood*. This juxtaposition of modern technology with classical art illustrates the Plants' eclectic tastes.

The grand staircase on the first floor is flanked with electrified newel posts from France and a giltwood framed plate-glass mirror, so guests could check their appearance before entering the rotunda. This photograph was taken in 1926 by Burgert Brothers Photography of Tampa. (THCPLS.)

Henry Plant equipped the Tampa Bay Hotel with two Otis elevators, one for passengers (pictured) and a freight elevator directly behind it. Originally, they operated with a hydraulic lift and were converted to electricity in the 1920s. The ornately carved doors of Spanish mahogany could be viewed from the corridor. The elevator serviced four floors. A partial fifth floor could be accessed via stairs. (THCPLS.)

The hotel offered and advertised many different amenities to please each and every guest. This view shows the hairdressing and manicure parlor that was part of the public rooms on the first floor. Victorian etiquette required ladies and gentlemen to be well-groomed and always look their best.

The card rooms in the bar and billiard area of the hotel were located in the basement and were for both ladies and gentlemen to enjoy. These less formal public spaces were accessed by stairs in the writing and reading room, the rotunda, or through an exterior entrance.

The writing and reading room, with inlays and ebony finishes, showed a masculine influence. This was a comfortable space reserved for men. A similar parlor off the rotunda was for the exclusive use of female guests. The museum has preserved the original objects from this room and restored the space to its original 1890s appearance.

The door to the left of the mantle in the writing and reading room led downstairs to the café, bar, and billiard rooms. Historic paint analysis revealed the original calcimine paint, and conservation efforts have restored the walls and cove moldings to the original golden-yellow color. The writing and reading room is the most historically accurate room in the entire building today.

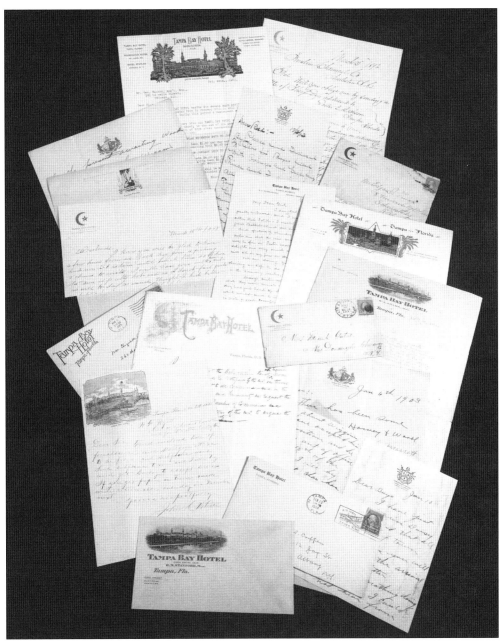

The hotel had its own print shop that produced letterhead, envelopes, and stationery for guests' use. Each manager selected a new design for his tenure at the hotel, and some included their names on the letterhead. Pictured are examples of a variety of hotel stationery.

This 1892 photograph shows a view of the grand salon filled with giltwood and inlaid furniture. Hotel advertisements described it as a "jewel casket" containing beautiful pieces. The wool carpet was scarlet red with lions. Legend has it that the carpet was made for and then refused by Queen Victoria because the figures resembled a lion rampant, the symbol of the British monarch. This photograph is part of the Gem Series by O. Pierre Havens.

Historic paint analysis revealed that the mantlepieces in the grand salon were white with gold leaf accents. The baseboards were also white and trimmed with 24-karat gold leaf. On January 29, 1891, the *Tampa Journal* newspaper reported that "decorators are at work putting the finishing touches of gilt on the handsome mantels." In 2016, the mantels and floor were restored to their original 1891 appearance.

The Marie Antoinette Divan is shown in this view from one of Plant's promotional booklets from 1893. The areas between the seats held potted plants. The room is filled with many chairs; perhaps this might be so that Victorian etiquette could be followed, and no one would need to sit on a seat that was still warm from the last occupant.

This stereoscopic view from 1898 shows the grand salon. Victorian style dictated that more was better, and this room was the perfect example of conspicuous consumption. It was crowded with bric-a-brac, furnishings, and ample seating for nearly 100 guests. From this room, guests could see the train arrivals and departures. Many of these furnishings are now part of the museum's permanent collection.

The music room, a curved and domed room just off the rotunda, had an electrified star on the ceiling and a ring of lights in the dome to add extra brightness and atmosphere to the room. The seven-paneled polyptych painting served as a backdrop for the hotel orchestras. During the Victorian era, social etiquette had strict rules for men and women to follow. It is said that the balconies were reserved for unescorted ladies to observe entertainments while maintaining Victorian standards of propriety.

Giovanni Tallarico's Orchestra played in the music room of the Tampa Bay Hotel during the 1909 season. Music was a regular part of the hotel atmosphere, with daily morning and afternoon concerts for the enjoyment of the guests.

Several thousand people received invitations to the Tampa Bay Hotel opening ball held on February 5, 1891. The *Tampa Daily Journal* reported that the hotel was "ablaze" with electric lights, Chinese lanterns, and fairy candles. "Throngs of people crowded the bridge . . . just to witness the illumination which was unquestionably one of the finest of the kind ever made."

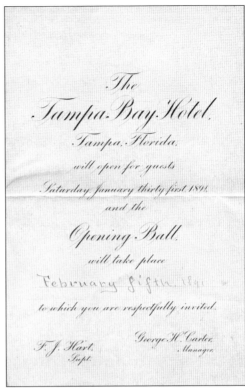

This February 5, 1891, opening night dance card with its original pencil and string attached shows the order of the dances and includes spaces to fill in the names of dance partners. The Tampa Bay Hotel Orchestra, under the direction of D.H. Stubblebine, provided the music for the grand event.

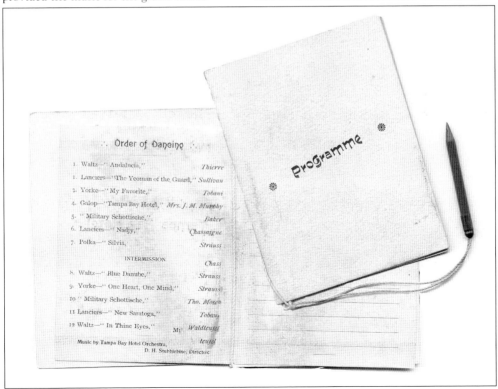

Those who attended the opening ball received favors that included fans for the ladies, crumb trays, and match strikers for the gentlemen. Carranza & Brothers of Havana, Cuba, made the fans for the occasion. Each one was hand-painted with alligators on the wooden slats and an image of the hotel surrounded by a silver horseshoe and seven jewels for good luck on the paper. (RRG.)

The finest accommodations in the hotel, known as the parlor suites, were located in each of the building's four corners. They contained three to seven adjoining rooms. The parlor suites on the first floor facing the garden were the most sought-after rooms as they had private entrances leading to the gardens. Margaret Plant is sitting in her private office in room 149 around 1893. Her face is reflected in the highly polished desktop.

This c. 1891 photograph by O. Pierre Havens shows the private parlor of Henry and Margaret Plant. The Plants' suite was on the first floor in the center of the hotel, now the University of Tampa's president's offices. The rooms overlooked the power plant and the Hillsborough River.

The hotel's public rooms were located on the first floor. This gold room was so named for the finishes on the giltwood chairs, the gold-leaf frames, and the ormolu-trimmed tables. Metal busts of Mary Queen of Scots and Cleopatra enhanced the setting. Large pocket doors at the right could be opened and closed for privacy. This view is from around 1926.

The solarium, a 150-foot curved corridor leading from the first-floor guest rooms to the dining room, abounded with live plants, whimsical garden stools, and marble inlaid chairs and tables. The Florida sun poured into the solarium through the large double-hung windows, creating a brightly lit, warm space in the hotel on chilly winter days.

This 1901 stereoscopic view shows the horseshoe-shaped arch at the entrance to the solarium. Potted palms and other tropical plants created a verdant greenhouse atmosphere simulating a garden effect inside. Many of the Chinese chairs and tables, ceramic jardinières, and over 40 of the original garden seats that accented the solarium are now part of the museum's permanent collection.

The dining room was designed to surround guests in opulent luxury and stimulate the senses. The hotel set tables with a mix of patterns for an aesthetic feast. A hotel brochure from the 1906–1907 season stated that it was "remarkable for its stately proportions . . . the effort has been toward space and dignity rather than toward crowding great numbers into limited accommodations." (THCPLS.)

These dishes were used in the dining room. They were made in England by Dunn Bennett and Company in the Ravenscliffe and Coronation patterns and have gold trim. They were a gift to the museum from Hortense Ford, daughter of the hotel doctor, Dr. Louis Oppenheimer. He served the hotel and was known for making house calls in his horse and buggy.

A Happy New Year

DINNER

Canape Caviar Bellevue

Cream of Chicken Fromentine aux Croutons Souffle
Bouillon en Tasse   Consomme Massena
Olives   Celery   Sweet Gherkins

Filet of Flounder Poached with White Wine Sauce Miss Paulette

Potatoes Brioche

Boiled Smoked Beef Tongue, Port Maillot

Contre Filet de Boeuf Pique a l'Americaine
Riz de Veau Braise a la Marechale
Scallop de Volaille, Tampa Bay
Peaches Melba Milady Sauce

Punch au Marasquin

Roast Ribs of Prime Beef au Jus
Roast Stuffed Country Turkey, Cranberry Sauce

Boiled New Potatoes   Mashed Potatoes
French Peas Sante au Beurre   Summer Squash
Oyster Bay Asparagus, Hollandaise   Steamed Rice
Browned Sweet Potatoes

Grape Fruit Salad

Steamed Citron Pudding, Brandy Sauce
Mince Pie   Pumpkin Pie
Vanilla Ice Cream   Charlotte Russe
Raisin Cake   Assorted Cake

Oranges   Bananas   Grapes   Apples   Tangerines

Mixed Nuts   Cluster Raisins   Dates   Figs

Cheese —   American   Roquefort   Edam
Saltines   Hard Water Crackers

Cafe Demi Tasse

TAMPA BAY HOTEL Some feed   Monday, Jan. 1, 1912.
H. M. STANFORD, Mgr.

Many local organizations used the dining room to host large events. Pictured is the Maas Brothers department store annual banquet held on January 14, 1925. Ladies are wearing the stylish 1920s cloche hats, flapper dresses, and bobbed hairstyles. The popular department store began in Tampa in 1886 and served the area until 1991. (THCPLS.)

The hotel print shop produced daily menus for the dining room. An 1894 *Tatler* magazine describes the dining experience: "A menu card, in keeping with the splendor surrounding me, was put in my hands . . . when the dinner came, a thin slice of rare beef on a charming bit of French porcelain; salad, on the reproduction of an old Vienna plate . . . an ice on a dear little plate . . . held an exquisite ice cream, coffee came in a beautiful Wedgwood cup."

Between 1910 and 1932, the hotel used a heavy stoneware hallmarked Grindley Hotel Ware, England. The dishes were plain white with a simple green ivy border and pink accent flowers. The silver flatware inscribed with the hotel name was made by the International Silver Company and Gorham Manufacturing. Sprawling place settings created an impressive visual effect that reinforced refined upbringing. Only those groomed in society could deftly navigate the proper etiquette associated with each piece.

The breakfast room was opposite the larger and more grand dining room. Here, guests and servants enjoyed an intimate setting for breakfast, lunch, or tea. This was also a preferred space for children and their nannies. The tables were set with Grindley Hotel Ware. This view is from a 1914 brochure that lists W.F. Adams as the hotel manager.

This 1905 view shows the hotel kitchen and staff with renowned chef Jules Bole (second from left). Some of the nation's most celebrated chefs ran the kitchen, overseeing at least two dozen workers, and determined the menus for the hotel, including Joseph P. Campazzi, Theodore Lamanna, and Emile Combe. The *New York Observer and Chronicle* noted that "The [hotel] food is cooked as well as at a private club, and served on choice porcelain with fine linen."

This rare interior view of the hotel bakery shows Oscar E. Skinner, steward (seated), with the bakery and pastry staff in 1905. Like the stewards who served before and after him, he assumed responsibility for the dining room's acclaimed epicurean experience. This photograph illustrates the subtle yet distinct division between the management (seated, wearing a suit) and the working class standing in their uniforms.

These copper-clad skillets and sauce pot were used in the kitchen. This was the finest cookware in America at the time, manufactured by Duparquet Huot Moneuse of New York. All three pieces bear the "T.B.H." monogram on the side.

This original wine crate with hand lettering was found in the ceiling crawl space above the dining room in the early 1990s. It contained one empty bottle of Barton and Gustier's Bordeaux and the straw packing sleeves used for padding the bottles during shipping.

DEAN CRANE DINNER
CORNELL UNIVERSITY ———
ASSOCIATION-OF-FLORIDA
TAMPA BAY HOTEL MARCH 7, 192

As an event space, the breakfast room was favored for smaller meetings, dinners, and special events that called for a more intimate space than the larger dining room. Pictured is the Dean Crane Dinner of the Cornell University Association of Florida, held on March 7, 1925. (MKL.)

Three

Strolling in a Perfect Paradise

Prior to 1800, ornamental gardens were a luxury enjoyed by royalty or the wealthy. Two key occurrences in the mid-1800s resulted in the rise of public parks and gardens. The debut of the Crystal Palace at the Great Exhibition of 1851 in London ignited an obsession for collecting exotic plants and displaying them in greenhouses or decorative gardens. Simultaneously, a growing social conscience for public well-being and quality of life led to the establishment of public parks. In 1853, the state of New York designated 750 acres to establish the United States' first landscaped public greenspace, which would become Central Park. Henry Plant lived on Fifth Avenue, a few blocks from Central Park. The public's positive response to this vast, cultivated open space influenced Plant's decision to develop a large decorative garden for the enjoyment of his guests.

Henry Plant selected the sloping lawn between the east front of the hotel and the Hillsborough River for his tropical paradise. The garden's design reflected the blending of historic designs, the Victorian penchant for the eclectic, and an understanding of tourists' expectations of exotic Florida. Plant drew inspiration from French, English, and Victorian styles for the 60-acre garden. The Classic French style emphasized manicured lawns and allées and required an elevated terrace from which to appreciate the grounds. The sweeping hotel veranda provided just such a vantage point. The English style sprinkled visually interesting and unexpected arrangements throughout the greenspace. Follies, fountains, garden ornamentation, and carefully selected plants that alluded to mythology, poetry, and literature were common elements. For a Victorian garden, an abundance of flowers and symmetrical beds were key elements. Plant traveled to Cuba and Jamaica with the hotel's head gardener, Anton Fiehe, to gather rare tropical plants. They returned to Tampa with a variety of specimens unequaled in the United States. Plant and Fiehe blended these landscape styles and collections to create a visually stimulating outdoor oasis. The Tampa Bay Hotel's garden was touted as the most exotic garden in the country.

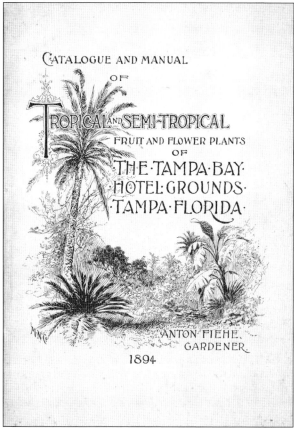

Guests staying on the east side of the building would have this view of the garden. This c. 1892 photograph by O. Pierre Havens shows many of the unique garden features including the "Tampa Bay Hotel" flowerbed (pictured here and opposite), flagpole, star-shaped bed, shell pathways, fountain, and Hydriotic Esplanade. Downtown Tampa is visible on the opposite bank of the Hillsborough River.

Plant personally selected Anton Fiehe to design, install, and maintain the hotel grounds. He served in that capacity from 1891 to 1905. It was said that Fiehe "paints pictures with life's real things." He wrote a 45-page catalog of all the plants on the grounds, published in 1892 and again in 1894. There are no known written plans for the landscape design, only photographs of the finished creation.

In 1891, William Drysdale wrote that walking the grounds was a "stroll in a fairyland." He noted walking "across the soft grass, past flower beds, fountains, palms, banana plantations, and beds of pineapples, toward the river." He passed by immense beds of violets, pansies, fragrant roses, clusters of oleanders, and bamboos. He "stood under the palmettos by the river [from] whence one of the best views of the building is to be had."

Plant erected a 100-foot tall flagpole in the center of the lawn. Atop the pole was "a gilt crescent, set with glass jewels, through which an incandescent light shines like a brilliant star at night." Purportedly, the light could be seen for several miles out in Tampa Bay. The *Plant System Budget* reported in 1895 that "a flagstaff floats the country's colors by day and sports a crescent of electric fire at night."

Historical postcards provide a visual record of the hotel and grounds. The messages they bear tell the stories of guests' experiences at the hotel. This undated card reads, "Dear Sister and Brother—This AM after breakfast Jay and I walked down this promenade and talked of our wedding day 17 years ago today. I picked a few sweet-scented violets and tried to remember all this lovely spot to tell you of later. . . . Love from all."

Margaret and Henry Plant are pictured in front of the hotel in rickshaws pulled by uniformed porters. Their uniforms sport a "TBH" monogram on the lapel and brass buttons bearing the Plant System logo. During the 1890s, African American men from New York worked seasonally in the hotel as porters, with additional workers recruited from Tampa's African American and Cuban communities.

An early Tampa Bay Hotel brochure states that the "most famous of the treasures in the garden is the magnificent live oak tree, under which tradition says, Spanish explorer [Hernando] De Soto camped when he first landed on this coast. What . . . would be his amazement could he behold . . . the splendid palace of hospitality whose walls are brushed by the spreading branches of this hoary, moss-hung tree?" This photograph was taken by J.C. Field around 1892.

On January 31, 1892, the *New York Times* commented on the lush and thriving grass. It noted that the hotel gardeners had demonstrated "that a beautiful green lawn can be made and maintained in the white sand of South Florida . . . roots of Bermuda grass were set out close together over the whole area. . . . I doubt whether the music of the lawn mower was ever heard south of St. Augustine before this lawn was made."

Tampa photographer William A. Fishbaugh took this photograph of the impressive De Soto Oak around 1910. The grand live oak still stands and remains a popular focal point of the grounds.

During the winter months, visitors arrived from the north to enjoy Florida's mild climate. One visitor identified only as FWG sent a postcard to Bessie Barrus of Bristol, Connecticut: "This is much better than snow drifts to me—but I suppose I shall have to take up the snow shovel again next week. Am VERY ANXIOUS to do so."

This photograph appeared in a promotional brochure titled "The Tampa Bay Hotel" advertising the 1910–1911 season. Two hotel porters are pulling guests about the gardens in rickshaws. Pictures from different years show the various styles of rickshaws that were used on the grounds. It is unknown why Plant had rickshaws at the hotel, but they reflected the Victorian fascination with Asian culture.

Wooden benches, identical to those used in Central Park, were placed along the pathways throughout the garden. The benches invited guests to pause during their stroll about the grounds and enjoy the tropical plants and garden sculptures, as this man is doing in 1908.

Sprinkled throughout the garden, a variety of garden seats provided a perch for guests who might become a bit breathless from the exertions of strolling—particularly the corseted ladies. The Plants brought garden seats from Japan, England, and Germany. As functional and decorative ceramic statues, they added a touch of elegance to the grounds.

A selection of fanciful garden stools modeled as a frog, monkey, toadstool, and a pillow-top seat added whimsey to the garden. In 1894, Arabella Hambleton, a young guest, noted in her diary that "The walk to the hotel was paved and along the sides were garden seats in china making it very beautiful."

In Victorian landscapes, the lawn was the centerpiece. Large estate lawns were manicured with gang mowers drawn by horses. The push mower, for smaller lawns, was patented during Queen Victoria's reign. At the Tampa Bay Hotel, the lawn was "carefully kept and green as one of Kentucky's own." A large roller, drawn by a mule, was used to keep it tidy and manageable. (LOC.)

An English-style garden feature was the folly, a landscape oddity—an out of place, unexpected discovery—meant to spark conversation among the guests as they strolled about the grounds. Plant salvaged two cannons from old Fort Brooke in Tampa and placed them in the garden as a Spanish fort folly. This photograph is dated 1903.

The landscape of the garden was not static; elements were regularly added or removed. Following Henry Plant's death in 1899, the fountain *Transportation* by sculptor George Grey Barnard was commissioned as a tribute to him.

As reported in the September 1902 issue of *House and Garden, Transportation* is a wall fountain, not meant to be viewed from the rear. It is strategically placed to be appreciated from the veranda. The streams of water that spray from the mouths of the fish are "veritable lines of composition, and they give breadth and reach to the design." This group of tourists poses before the notable sculpture during the 1910–1911 season.

Anna F. Labadie and her parents pause in front of *Transportation* around 1914. The sculpture includes a steamship on the upper left and a locomotive on the upper right, elements symbolizing the Plant System of transportation. An eagle with a strongbox is perched on top, representing Plant's first company, the Southern Express Company. The work honors Plant's development of a vast transportation network.

The message on the back of this photograph muses, "Not another soul in the world but me." After the hotel closed in 1932, the building, grounds, and *Transportation* continued to be a popular backdrop for photographs. In 1933, the Tampa Municipal Museum (now the Henry B. Plant Museum) and the University of Tampa were established in the former Tampa Bay Hotel.

In 1901, the *Morning Tribune* described one garden feature: "a cone of rock with jets of crystal water spurting from the top and sides and falling into a basin as a beautiful and refreshing sight." Colored electric lights, fairy lights, or Japanese lanterns illuminated the sparkling cone-shaped fountain. By 1911, the formation was dubbed the Jewel Box and Tea Garden. The pyramid of small boulders was covered with chips of colored glass that sparkled in the sun. This delightful setting became a popular backdrop for ladies' tea parties and social activities.

This c. 1933 view of a reflecting pool is a hand-painted watercolor found in a private scrapbook. Historians and master gardeners believe that this area was originally one of the fountains that was later converted into a shallow pond with beautiful water lilies. Today, a contemporary sculpture, *Sticks of Fire* by O.V. Shaffer, stands in this location.

Ernest Maas Sr. stands amidst bamboo plants on the grounds of the Tampa Bay Hotel in 1908. The bamboo garden was another example of a Victorian collection of tropical plants. The inclusion of bamboo reflected the eclectic and worldly design of the garden, as it evoked impressions of China or Japan.

Stereoscopic views were popular in the 19th century. They contained a brief caption or description and the publishing company information. This 1907 card is entitled "Under the Bamboo Tree, Tampa, Florida, U.S.A." Images of children on the hotel grounds were rare. This stereo card is part of a unique series that features six little girls posing in various locations about the garden.

William Drysdale wrote, "There is a gentle slope . . . to the river, and near the top of the ascent a spring of pure water bubbles from the ground, and runs in a little streamlet to the shore. The moist sides of this brook have been converted into a tropical jungle, full of palms, bananas, flowers, and ferns." Advertised as having "famous" healing qualities, this freshwater creek still runs through the garden. It originates from a spring underneath the hotel. This photograph is from around 1933.

A c. 1896 Tampa Bay Hotel brochure advertises an attractive garden feature: "Beside the river leading to the Casino and the boathouse is the famous palmetto walk where the big trees clasp hands overhead, making quite the most romantic lover's lane imaginable." Today, the scenic palm walk attracts thousands of visitors annually. It is part of Tampa's West River Trail. (LOC.)

Ruoy H. Cason, his father, P.H. Cason (Tampa city engineer), and George W. Bean pose along the palm walk around 1910. The renowned palm, or palmetto, walk, lined with sabal palms (Florida's state tree), stretched along the bank of the Hillsborough River. It was the quintessential pathway for strolling, a scenic avenue shaded by overlapping palm branches. The walk led to the Hydriotic Esplanade, boat slips, and docks.

This postcard shows guests enjoying the palm walk along the edge of the Hillsborough River. The palm walk followed a portion of the garden's 2,000-foot-long riverfront. Postmarked February 8, 1925, and addressed to Lillian Babbitt of Thompson, Connecticut, the message reads, "We are far away from home and having a fine time in sunny Florida. The weather is wonderful. Charlie caught one fish today weighing 70 pounds. Lovingly, Mrs. Ross."

This stereo card entitled "A Date Palm in Tampa Bay Park, Tampa, U.S.A." was produced by the H.C. White Company. This image also appears in the hotel's 1910–1911 season brochure, which lists David Lauber as the manager.

Fiehe's use of tropical plants, especially palms, and playfully shaped flowerbeds made the Tampa Bay Hotel garden one of the most enchanting in the nation. Influenced by the Eclectic Style of landscape design, he created an exotic paradise to complement the mysterious Moorish Revival architecture of the hotel. A 1907 advertisement described the grounds: "Scarlet hibiscus, glorious poinsettias, roses and lilies are here. Curious delightful shrubs from Japan; arbor vitae runs riot, and all the wonders of a tropic Garden of Eden."

From left to right, Cora Morris and Clarence and Bertha Jackson from Ontario, Canada, pose in front of the hotel. The flowerbed before them illustrates "bedding out," or filling flowerbeds with one type of flower to create a uniform expanse. This was a popular planting style during the Victorian era. Fiehe used this style for many of the beds around the hotel.

This patch of garden adds a lush accent to the bricked walkway in front of the hotel. Over the years, different plants grew in this section of the garden. In this photograph, papayas and herbs are used instead of flowering plants. Ripe fruit and the smell of herbs stimulated the senses of hotel guests as they strolled. In the dining room, the menus featured tropical foods found growing about the grounds, an early example of farm-to-table cuisine.

Marjorie Stoneman Douglas recalled traveling to Florida in 1894 when she was four years old. She had a vivid memory of being lifted up to pick an orange off a tree on the hotel grounds. Pictured here are the orange groves on the property.

Bertha Jackson (left) and Cora Morris stand beside a palm tree and fountain. Morris's hat is adorned with feathers, the highest of fashions for the late 19th and early 20th centuries. Florida played an instrumental role in the fashion industry as a source of exotic feathers. The great demand for feathers nearly drove many species of birds to extinction and led to the founding of today's National Audubon Society.

This view of the promenade between the hotel and garden was painted by artist Olive Commons (1880–1963). Commons arrived in Florida in 1908. Inspired by the state's natural beauty, she hand-painted Florida scenes on porcelain medallions set in jewelry mountings as gifts for friends. The "cameonas," as she called them, became so popular with locals and tourists, she started a cottage industry that eventually grew to include hand-painted dinnerware.

From left to right, Fred and Cora Morris stand with Bertha Jackson in the garden. Over the years, the garden design changed. Some of the ground was lost when the casino was built in 1896. By 1911, most of the flowerbeds and vegetable gardens had been replaced with open lawns. In 1913, an article in *Life* magazine wrote that the garden had 42 acres of "luxuriant tropical shrubbery and flowers, beautiful palm fringed walks, fountains and shady nooks, facing the Hillsborough River."

Au Coup de Fusil (At the Ready) is a bronze patina sculpture of hunting dogs by artist Églantîne Lemaitre (1852–1920), one of the few female sculptors whose work gained recognition during her lifetime. It was cast in France in 1890 by Maurice Denonvilliers. Installed on the grounds in 1891 as the first piece of public art in Tampa, the sculpture greeted guests as they arrived by train at the hotel's west front. Today, *Au Coup de Fusil* welcomes visitors as they enter the Henry B. Plant Museum.

This historical postcard of the east front shows the long bricked promenade with tropical landscaping. Postmarked December 4, 1906, it is addressed to Mrs. W.H. Tomble of Pittsford, Vermont. The message reads, "Snow and ice strictly forbidden on these premises. Cousin Will."

Alsey Sanders, seen around 1900, is standing with a statue of a large bird on the edge of the garden by the east entrance to the hotel. The Henry B. Plant Museum is fortunate to have a number of original Tampa Bay Hotel objects in the permanent collection. Regrettably, this piece has been lost to time.

The grounds boasted three glasshouse conservatories for the cultivation of tropical plants. This c. 1895 postcard shows one of the conservatories in the center, with the light-colored dome. The innovative Crystal Palace in London influenced the popularity of greenhouses. For the first time, plants could survive in freezing weather. The *New York Times* noted in 1891 that "There were certainly enough flowers then in bloom in the conservatory to supply all the hotels in Florida."

Tampa Bay Hotel, from Water Front, Tampa, Fla.

The garden was designed as a pleasure to experience while strolling or viewing from an elevated vantage point. The eclectic designs drew attention to displays of exotic plants and enticed visitors with surprising touches such as flowerbeds shaped like stars, hearts, or an anchor. One charming feature was the Owl, so named because when the pathway was viewed from above, it resembled a bird's head in profile. Today, a little over six acres of the original park remain.

Four

Sports, Amusements, and Around the Grounds

The Gilded Age, noted for conspicuous consumption, or the display of wealth and power, saw a rise in recreational sports and amusements because the wealthy class had the time and money to participate in leisure activities. With 150 acres at his disposal, Henry Plant created a lavish destination resort dedicated to the enjoyment of such experiences. Hotel amusements included the newest trends in indoor and outdoor diversions. By the 1890s, Americans were enamored with tennis, croquet, bowling, bicycling, baseball, and golf. Plant established areas for each of these entertainments, along with accommodations for boating, musical and dramatic entertainments, swimming, hunting, fishing, racing, cards, and billiards. At the Tampa Bay Hotel, there was no shortage of ways to fill a day in paradise; it was a luxurious 19th-century playground.

Plant's resort offered amusements for everyone—from blood-pumping outdoor sports to more refined and cultural indoor entertainments. Some diversions capitalized on Florida's natural attributes such as tropical wilderness, miles of coastline, and a warm climate for hunting, fishing, and swimming. During the 1890s, resort hotels were defining themselves as tournament venues. Attuned to these trends, Plant installed a world-class golf course, tennis courts, racetrack, and baseball diamond. Guests could take pleasure in the sports themselves or watch lively competitions. In the 1920s, attendance at spring training for professional baseball teams became a popular pastime for all ages.

Luxury resorts were also evolving as spa destinations touting the latest curative amenities. In 1896, Plant opened the new Tampa Bay Casino. Primarily a performance hall lauded as one of the finest playhouses outside of New York City, the casino featured a natatorium and spa. A c. 1900 hotel brochure announced a recent addition that would make the hotel "rank among the most famous health resorts of the world" was the establishment of a "complete hydrotherapeutic plant."

Plant appreciated music and theater and brought those elements to the hotel and Tampa. For the casino stage, he engaged world-class musicians and performers for the enjoyment of his guests and the community. Through the array of dramatic, musical, dance, and oratorical programs in the casino and the daily musical concerts in the hotel's music room, Plant brought culture to Tampa and laid the foundation for the city's future support of the arts and culture.

Plant System passenger traffic agent B.W. Wrenn managed all marketing and promotion for the Plant transportation network. Under his supervision, advertisements were developed and distributed across North America. This Tampa Bay Hotel graphic appeared in national publications, such as *Life* magazine on February 7, 1901. Like many of the marketing materials, it promotes the lovely grounds, golf links, bicycle paths, hunting, fishing and boating, carriage rides, and the Hillsborough River. For advertising purposes, the artist inverted the "Tampa Bay Hotel" flower bed, which in reality faced the hotel windows.

The Plant System provided a number of local and international excursion opportunities embarking from the Tampa Bay Hotel. Guests seeking an extended pleasure trip could travel to Havana via a Plant System steamship. For shorter jaunts, a day trip to Picnic Island near Port Tampa was popular, a mere 30-minute train ride from the hotel. This c. 1893 promotional card touted the fishing, sailing, pleasant sea air, and bathing.

The Tampa Bay Hotel, with its exotic architecture, luxury accommodations, fashionable diversions, world renowned entertainers, and chefs on staff, had no shortage of attributes to attract tourists. This rare c. 1908 advertisement focuses on the curative climate and atmosphere of Florida's west coast for the benefit of "knotted Northern nerves" and mental health.

Victorians were fascinated with Asian culture, following the opening of Japan by Commodore Matthew Perry in 1854. Rickshaws, prevalent in many Asian cultures, were used around the hotel grounds. Pictured here around 1909, a Mr. Van Buren is pulling his wife. The other women are, from left to right, Minnie B. Lauber, wife of the hotel manager; Mrs. Merritt; and Nellie Harden Macfarlane.

Photographer J.D. Givens captured four young visitors in front of the hotel gates. The boy has an orange blossom branch in his mouth. The girl at center poses with her safety bicycle, and the sign in the background reads "Bicycles not allowed in hotel grounds." Although the garden pathways were off-limits, designated bicycle paths were available on the opposite side of the building.

This image from a glass-plate negative shows the Tampa Bay Hotel's east front. The sign "To the Boats" directs guests to the boathouse and Hydriotic Esplanade along the Hillsborough River. Hotel records indicate that 62 boats were launched in 1891, including 35 cedar yawls, six birchbark Indian canoes, two naptha launches, three sailing yachts, five sharpies, and 10 skiffs—all available for the guests' use.

In 1892, the *New York Times* reported, "The boating department is one of the most fertile sources of amusement about the hotel. The boathouse . . . is under the charge of Captain Warner, and I can testify from experience that it could not be in better or safer hands." According to the account, visitors kept Captain Warner busy with their desire to be on the water.

The sign at lower left warns "No Shooting Allowed," an indication that wildlife roamed just a few yards from the hotel's front doors. The 1895 hotel game record noted that on December 4, Mr. and Mrs. G.W. Bergner of Philadelphia killed 283 snipe and plover, one yellow-leg, two willets, and one duck, breaking a guest record.

Arthur Schleman was engaged as the hotel sporting guide for many years. He took guests hunting for deer, birds, bears, bobcats, alligators, and smaller animals. As a young correspondent, Winston Churchill traveled to Cuba via Tampa and acquired Schleman's business card. The card listed his rates as $4 per day for a guide and dogs and $1 for a gun, with no charge for the hunting coat, boots, and leggings.

Henry Plant heavily promoted Florida's sporting opportunities and produced an illustrated publication entitled *Gun and Rod on the West Coast of Florida* that described the game and fish to be found in the area. He is pictured with a tarpon caught near Fort Myers, Florida, during the 1890s. (SFHS.)

Margaret Plant also participated in Florida's outdoor activities. She is shown here with her catch of the day. On another occasion in 1893, she organized a fishing party with the family of the future US secretary of war Russell A. Alger on the steamer *Margaret*. The *New York Times* reported, "Off Egmont Key they took in thirty minutes, 503 pounds of fish." (SFHS.)

83

This is the cover of an advertising leaflet promoting golf and various leisure activities at the hotel. Henry Plant hired John Hamilton Gillespie to design an 18-hole golf links and to teach guests the increasingly popular game. In 1901, the course hosted the Florida Golf Association tournament.

A golfing party is pictured on the edge of the golf course with the hotel's minarets visible in the background. Some of the people pictured are Mrs. Durrett, Dr. R.D. Small, Helen Dick (wife of the hotel manager), Miss C. Harding, Harry Rawlins, L.C. Serves, W.E. Buclock, Millie Smith, Tom Dunn, A.E. Dick (manager), George Lorr, and John Hamilton Gillespie (in center with golf bag). (RC.)

In March 1892, the hotel hosted the first annual Gulf Coast Championship tournament of the Tampa Bay Lawn Tennis Club. Dr. James Dwight, the father of American tennis, was the referee. This photograph was taken around that time. Plant invited amateur tennis players to come to the opening of the Tampa Bay Hotel in the early 1890s. Rising tennis star John W. Nichols traveled with Plant in his private railcar for this occasion and was a guest at the hotel.

This stereoscopic view shows the tennis court with a game underway. The players are dressed in white long-sleeved shirts and white trousers, the mandated color for playing tennis. According to *Wright and Ditson's Lawn Tennis Guide* of 1892, the hotel's cement courts "were pronounced by all to be the finest courts in Florida."

This c. 1902 scene of guests playing croquet is from a Tampa Bay Hotel travel brochure. The sport of croquet originated in Europe in the mid-19th century. The game quickly gained favor as an amusement during garden parties.

The hotel was advertised in national publications to promote tourism to Florida and to entice guests to spend their holidays here. Highlighting the popular experience of motor car touring, the hotel offered a choice selection of automobiles at the disposal of guests, complete with a skilled chauffeur. The available choices were the luxury brands Pierce-Arrow, Stearns, or White.

These men are about to set out for an afternoon automobile tour in a 1903 Oldsmobile Curved Dash Runabout. Built between 1901 and 1907 by the Olds Motor Works, the Curved Dash Oldsmobile was the first mass-produced automobile. It was the bestselling car in America from 1902 to 1905 and cost $650. This was rather expensive at a time when the average annual wage was $489.

Minnie Mosley Farnsworth and guests are pictured in a 1905 Buick on the west front of the hotel. A historical postcard from the museum's archives dated February 22, 1913, sent to S. Catherine Poor of West Newburg, Massachusetts, reads, "This hotel is exquisitely grand. Never saw anything as beautiful before. The parlor is a dream. So are the corridors, writing rooms, etc. . . . Had a moonlight auto ride by the water last night. Grand! Love, Sis."

The grounds of the Tampa Bay Hotel were a playground for guests and the residents of Tampa alike. People strolled through the expansive gardens enjoying the exotic landscaping. Many of them posed for photographs using the unusual architecture and tropical setting as a memorable backdrop. Pictured here are Alice Pearl Haynes Evans (left) and her sister Eva Evans Gebhart around 1920.

Over the years, various animals were housed in the garden. The hotel advertised raccoon and monkey houses, and peacocks roamed the grounds. A 1905 hotel inventory published in the *Tampa Weekly Tribune* notes, "An alligator named Joe and a monkey named Dan" were among the items on the property. In the late 1930s a bear was added to the menagerie, which became known as the "zoo" in the garden. In 1957, they were relocated and became the core of what is now ZooTampa at Lowry Park.

From left to right, George W. Bean and P.H. and Ruoy Cason examine the cannon folly around 1910. The cannons were originally used at Fort Brooke, established in 1824 and located in what is now downtown Tampa. Plant moved the cannons to the hotel grounds and incorporated them into a classic folly, featuring the "remains" of an old Spanish fort. This folly remains in its garden location today.

Plant's garden folly received a great deal of interest, and the *New York Times* commented on January 31, 1892, "In the center of the grounds, between the hotel and the river, is a large fountain, and near it a miniature fort, on which are mounted several rusty guns." James C. Stuart from Lancaster, Ohio, was a photographer for the Tampa Bay Hotel around the turn of the 20th century. He is pictured with the garden folly in 1903.

The hotel's park became known as Plant Park, the first in Tampa's municipal park system. Tampa embraced Plant Park and held many social and civic events on the public greenspace, such as musical concerts, Easter services, and theatrical productions, as seen here on May 15, 1922. (THCPLS.)

For those guests who enjoyed being out of doors, but not the vigor of the hunt, the garden offered a natural and exotic experience. On March 24, 1923, the Burgert Brothers documented a party in the tea garden. Also known as the Jewel Box, the cone-shaped fountain was a dazzling setting as the iridescent rocks sparkled from the water and sunshine. Electric lights are strung above the fountain. (THCPLS.)

Bachman Band concerts were one of the many events held in the park. Harold Bachman was a prominent music educator and military band leader. This is the cover of the concert program for the week of March 29, 1925, announcing "The Tampa Board of Trade Presents: Bachman and his Million-Dollar Band." It was so named in 1917 after an Army general said his band was worth a million dollars to the US Army.

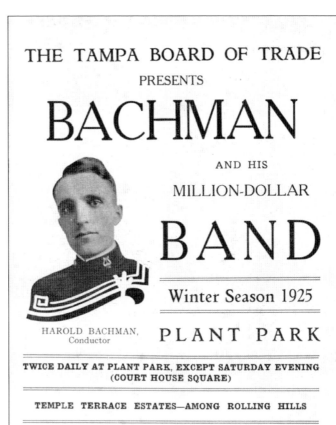

THE TAMPA BOARD OF TRADE

PRESENTS

BACHMAN

AND HIS

MILLION-DOLLAR

BAND

Winter Season 1925

HAROLD BACHMAN,
Conductor

PLANT PARK

TWICE DAILY AT PLANT PARK, EXCEPT SATURDAY EVENING
(COURT HOUSE SQUARE)

TEMPLE TERRACE ESTATES—AMONG ROLLING HILLS

Program For Week March 29th, 1925

TRIBUNE PUB. CO., TAMPA

Leslie's Weekly magazine featured the Tampa Bay Hotel Glee Club in the April 7, 1898, issue. Hotel waiters doubled as members of the Glee Club. "Billy Green" is pictured in the center. Minstrel shows and cakewalks performed by hotel employees were common in grand resorts in the South in the latter part of the 19th century.

Guests enjoyed musical entertainments at various locations about the property. The hotel orchestra performed morning and afternoon concerts on the west veranda of the hotel. Guests spent many leisurely hours on the shaded veranda listening to the music.

Antoinette Robb (1885–1946), a classically trained cellist, played background music in the hotel dining room and at the Tampa Bay Casino. In the dining room, she and other musicians performed from the balcony above the diners. Their music reverberated off the large dome and drifted down into the dining room. In the casino, she performed on the stage.

In addition to all of the amenities and fabulous attention to detail, the hotel hosted special holiday dinners. An annual favorite was George Washington's birthday. The menus for these celebrations were particularly attractive, with colorful graphics and specialty dishes created for the occasion, such as Martha Washington Pie.

Many regional and national organizations held their banquets in the dining room, such as this festive 1927 Kiwanis event. In 1914, the hotel switched from staffing the dining room with African American male servers to white women, as seen here. (THCPLS.)

Henry Plant hired world-class musicians to delight guests at the hotel with daily concerts. This view shows the interior of the music room with a baby grand piano and a multi-paneled painting called *Wine, Women, and Song* as a backdrop for the hotel orchestras. Today, this original work hangs in the museum and a replica in the music room recreates the authentic atmosphere. (THCPLS.)

After Plant's death, the managers continued the tradition of selecting renowned musical entertainers for the season. Pictured is Giovanni Tallarico. He and his orchestra performed in the music room during the 1909 season.

The Tampa Bay Casino opened in 1896 as one of Tampa's earliest performance halls. According to newspaper accounts, it was to be an "oasis in the desert." International entertainers appeared on the stage of this renowned site. The casino also contained spa facilities and a swimming pool measuring 50 feet by 75 feet. The stage boards, a temporary wooden floor, could be taken up to reveal the spring-fed swimming pool underneath. The casino remained the centerpiece of Tampa's cultural life until it burned to the ground in 1941.

Performances at the casino were open to hotel guests as well as city residents. Pictured is the Tampa Bay Casino program from John Philip Sousa's February 3, 1922, concert. Other famous performers who appeared on the stage included operatic soprano Dame Nellie Melba in 1893; actor Madame Sarah Bernhardt, 1906; orator Booker T. Washington, 1912; prima ballerina Anna Pavlova, 1915; and pianist Ignace Paderewski, 1919.

A hotel advertisement noted that the casino had a "theatrical auditorium with a floor space larger than almost any New York theatre. Its stage was of spacious dimensions, and its settings were artistic and costly. The main floor was furnished with handsome opera chairs, providing seating for 2,000 persons." A number of the best theatrical companies were engaged each season and appeared at intervals, presenting only first-class attractions.

The casino's programs contained advertisements for local businesses and services and also promoted the available amenities, which included spa facilities. As noted on the cover of this program, guests were encouraged to try the hydro-therapeutic treatments in the spa's hydratic establishment.

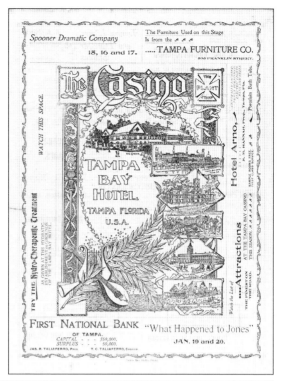

There are only a few known photographs showing the interior of the casino. This rare view shows a ballet performance in the 1920s. The tile walls beneath the stage were part of the swimming pool. (THCPLS.)

97

Fred Morris stands beside the bar and billiard room sign near the east front of the hotel. He and his family stayed at the hotel in the early 1900s. The directional signage helped guests navigate their way around the 150 acres of hotel property.

The hotel bar was located in the basement beneath the east veranda. Various advertisements and posters, including Plant's Southern Express Company and "Bloomer Girls . . . Baseball Club," decorated the walls. Today, this area is a sandwich shop known as the Rathskellar.

In the basement, several billiard tables filled the room adjacent to the bar. The large squares in the ceiling are the skylights from the east veranda that allowed natural light to supplement the hotel's modern, but dim electric lights. This photograph was taken around 1899.

This 1906 image shows the Hillsborough High School football team with their mascot dog seated on the steps of the hotel. The grounds were a gathering place for photo opportunities for guests and local residents alike.

The greenspace around the hotel was used for various lawn activities. This view shows a well-attended horseshoe tournament on the grounds in 1922. The gentlemen competitors are playing in their shirts, ties, and hats. They have removed their jackets and hung them from the tree trunks. (THCPLS.)

The golf course, race track, and exhibition buildings were located on the west side of the hotel property. Pictured here is the racing track. First used for horse racing, the track was later used for automobile and motorcycle racing. This open space was where Buffalo Bill Cody's Wild West show performed during his farewell tour in 1912.

Gasparilla, a local festival based on the legend of pirate Jose Gaspar, began on the hotel grounds in 1904. Over the years, Gasparilla evolved to include a coronation ball, sea invasion, and parades. To build interest in the early years, Gasparilla coincided with the state fair. This view captures the combined festivities in 1926. (THCPLS.)

This 1924 view shows just a portion of the grandiose display that was Gasparilla and the state fair. The race track and circus act are in the foreground, and the hotel's minarets are visible in the background. Eventually, these events outgrew the space. The parade moved to Bayshore Boulevard, and the fair moved to the new state fairgrounds in 1976. (THCPLS.)

Henry Plant actively promoted all of Florida's attributes. He constructed displays of Florida products to advertise the state's resources at the 1889 Exposition Universelle in Paris, the 1895 Cotton States and International Exposition in Atlanta, and the World's Columbian Exposition of 1893 in Chicago. He erected an exhibition hall (pictured here at left center) on the west side of the hotel to enable guests to view these Florida-themed promotional displays. These efforts brought Florida to the international community.

Five

THE HOTEL AND THE SPANISH-AMERICAN WAR

In 1895, Cuban revolutionaries began the Cuban War of Independence, the last of three rebellions to free the island from Spanish rule. The insurgents' strategy of destroying sugarcane fields threatened $50 million in US investments. Simultaneously, the Spanish policy of herding civilians into urban detention centers caused thousands of deaths from hunger and disease. This "reconcentration" program created tremendous support in the United States for humanitarian aid. A diplomatic crisis erupted after the explosion of the battleship USS *Maine* in Havana's harbor on February 15, 1898, which killed 266 servicemen under unclear circumstances. Spain rejected a US ultimatum to allow Pres. William McKinley to arbitrate the conflict between Cuba and Spain. In response, Congress declared war against Spain on April 25, 1898.

Tampa's large Cuban community had already taken up the call of "Cuba Libre," offering financial support and facilitating gunrunning operations to Cuba. Concerned that the city was vulnerable to Spanish attack, local and state officials sought federal aid to fortify Tampa Bay. Henry Plant wrote Secretary of War Russell Alger to request that he "remember Tampa" in the military's plan to protect Florida's coast.

Plant sent his top official, Franklin Q. Brown, to Washington, DC, to lobby for Tampa's selection as the port of embarkation for the US invasion of Cuba. Brown outlined how Plant's railroad and port operations in west-central Florida could provide continuous rail and steamship transportation for troops and supplies. The Tampa Bay Hotel offered comfortable lodging for officers, foreign attachés, dignitaries, and war correspondents. The appeal succeeded. Tampa became the point of embarkation, and the hotel became the headquarters of the US Army.

The war between the United States and Spain lasted 113 days, and the world's attention was focused on Tampa during this period. The city struggled to cope with the massive military build-up for the invasion. The influx of more than 30,000 troops tested the city's resources; Henry Plant's railroad, steamship, and port facilities; and the elegant Tampa Bay Hotel.

The war against Spain officially ended with the signing of the Treaty of Paris on December 10, 1898. The treaty recognized Cuba's independence from Spain as well as the US annexation of Spain's remaining possessions, including Guam, Puerto Rico, and the Philippines.

RAILWAYS.

SAVANNAH, FLORIDA & WESTERN.
CHARLESTON & SAVANNAH.
ALABAMA MIDLAND.
BRUNSWICK & WESTERN.
FLORIDA SOUTHERN.
SANFORD & ST. PETERSBURG.
SILVER SPRINGS, OCALA & GULF.
ST. JOHNS & LAKE EUSTIS.
ASHLEY RIVER.
GREEN POND, WALTERBORO & BRANCHVILLE.
ABBEVILLE SOUTHERN.
TAMPA & THONOTOSASSA.
WINSTON & BONE VALLEY.

Plant System

HOTELS.

TAMPA BAY.
PORT TAMPA INN.
SEMINOLE, WINTER PARK.
OCALA HOUSE, OCALA, FLA.
BELLEVIEW HOTEL, BELLEAIR, FLA.
KISSIMMEE, KISSIMMEE, FLA.

STEAMSHIP LINES.

PORT TAMPA, KEY WEST & HAVANA.
PORT TAMPA & MOBILE.
PORT TAMPA & ISLAND OF JAMAICA.
PORT TAMPA & MANATEE RIVER.
BOSTON & HALIFAX.
BOSTON, CAPE BRETON & PRINCE EDWARD ISLAND.
CHATTAHOOCHEE RIVER.
PUNTA GORDA & FORT MYERS.
PORT TAMPA & ST. PETERSBURG.

Tampa, Fla., March 22nd, 1898

Dear sir:-

In considering the present relations existing between our country, Spain and the Island of Cuba, I fear I should be recreant to my duty should I fail to advise you of the unprotected condition of Tampa Bay and vicinity.   Since your visit to Tampa, some years since, it has grown from a straggling village to a very considerable city of some 25,000 inhabitants.   The country hereabouts is rapidly filling up with emigrants from all parts of the United States, and, in case of hostilities, it would seemingly be an attractive object of attack by the enemy.

You will recollect that Egmont Island, or Key, stretches across the mouth of Tampa Bay a distance of about four miles from water sufficiently deep for the operations of any cruisers drawing 30 feet of water.   The main ship channel passes in at the North end of the Island, carrying about twenty two feet of water, and suf-ficiently deep for the White Squadron, under Admiral Walker, when wintering at Tampa Bay to pass in and out at pleasure.   The Southern channel passes in at the South end of the island, and both are very direct channels and perfectly practicable for vessels to pass in and out without other pilots than their own navigating officers.

Either of these channels could be easily protected was suf-ficient time given, but should protection be required in the immediate future, I should consider, as at present, the Bay would be entirely

In 1898, Tampa mayor Myron E. Gillette, Tampa's US representative Stephen M. Sparkman, and members of the Tampa Board of Trade wrote letters to the US War Department requesting military support for the defense of the city. Each individual outlined Tampa's vulnerable position and emphasized the significance of the area. On March 22, 1898, Henry Plant sent this letter to Secretary of War Russell Alger requesting military attention. (NA.)

defenceless unless it should be guarded by proper vessels of the Navy

The country North and South of Tampa Bay, fronting the Gulf of Mexico, and within the radius of fifty miles from the entrance to Tampa Bay, is rapidly filling up with inhabitants, and landings could be effected at various points. Telegraph facilities on both coasts which could be utilized to bring together a force to repel any probable attack, and Port Tampa is eligibly located and can be readily reached by boat to points South of the Bay via the Manatee River section; North of the entrance to the Bay by boat to St Petersburg thence by rail.

I feel constrained to give you these particulars, and earnestly urge that this location not be lost sight of by the officers of your Department.

Regretting I have not had the pleasure of meeting yourself and family during the present season, which under the circumstances, by the way, we could not expect,

I am,

Very truly yours,

Hon. Russell A. Alger,

Secretary of War,

Washington, D. C.

Plant wrote to Secretary Alger on Plant System letterhead. He explained the importance of defending Tampa Bay and outlined how the defense vessels might access the area. He closed his letter with a reference to their personal relationship, as the Algers had been guests of the Plants during a fishing excursion in 1893. (NA.)

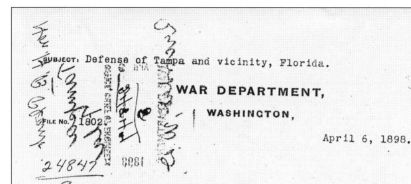

SUBJECT: Defense of Tampa and vicinity, Florida.

WAR DEPARTMENT,

WASHINGTON,

FILE No. 1802.

April 6, 1898.

My dear Sir:

    In further response to your letter of 22nd ultimo, urging the necessity of a more substantial defense of Tampa Bay and vicinity, Florida, I have the honor to inform you that the Chief of Engineers, to whom, as you were previously advised, the matter was referred, reports as follows:

> "Tampa Bay is not included in the list of harbors for which projects were prepared by the Endicott Board, but if it is the wish of the Secretary of War, immediate orders will be given the Board of Engineers to prepare a project and estimate of cost for its defense.

    Authority has been granted for the immediate preparation of a project and estimate of cost of this defense.

        Very respectfully,

              Secretary of War.

Mr. H. B. Plant,

    Tampa, Florida.

The chief of engineers's office responded to the Tampa officials' requests. The replies politely stated that the War Department could not possibly defend the entire Florida coast. Secretary Alger personally responded to Plant twice. The tone of Alger's April 6 letter indicates that Plant's personal relationship with Alger carried influence. Preparations to defend Tampa were announced on April 15 in front of the county courthouse in Tampa and were received with great celebration. (NA.)

THE   SPANISH-AMERICAN   WAR.

Hand-drawn sketches from the *Illustrated London News* of June 4, 1898, show five views of the mobilization at Tampa. They include a gun drill by the 5th Artillery, the 22nd Infantry with arms piled and ready to pitch tents, arrival in camp of the 22nd Infantry, the 1st Infantry passing through Tampa after a long practice march, and a group of Cuban recruits at Crespidas Hall in West Tampa. Author Trumbull White noted in 1898, "No such aggregation of light and heavy artillery has been gathered before at any one city in the United States, even in war time."

The Spanish-American War was the first time since the Civil War that Union and Confederate officers came together to serve in the US Army. Pictured from left to right are some of the officers who had official headquarters at the Tampa Bay Hotel: Col. J.B. Babcock, H. McKittrick, Brig. Gen. William Ludlow, Maj. J.W. Jacobs, Maj. Gen. William Rufus Shafter, Lt. John D. Miley, Lt. Col. C.F. Humphrey, and 1st Lt. R.H. Noble. General Wheeler (not pictured) served in the Confederate Cavalry, and General Shafter was a Union Army officer who received the Medal of Honor during the Civil War. (THCPLS.)

During the 1890s, the Tampa Bay Hotel closed for the summer from April to November. Henry Plant reopened the hotel in late April 1898 to accommodate Army headquarters. The *New York Times* reported on April 28, 1898, that the hotel was also open to the general public during this time. "The entire [hotel] staff of help, part of which was already on its way North, has been recalled, and the house will be kept open until the necessities of war shall have passed." (TRC.)

The government began dispatching regiments to Tampa beginning in April 1898. Thousands of soldiers continued to arrive throughout June. As regiments arrived in town, their commanding officers scouted and selected areas for camps. Troop encampments were established in West Tampa, Port Tampa City, and to the north and east of downtown Tampa. (HD.)

Correspondents representing major newspapers from around the world arrived in Tampa. Posing on the hotel's steps are some of the prominent war correspondents of the era. From left to right are writer and illustrator Frederic Remington, correspondent for *Harper's Weekly* magazine; Caspar Whitney (seated); Grover Flint (seated in profile); Richard Harding Davis (standing in white trousers); and Capt. Arthur H. Lee (standing), from Great Britain.

Between April and June 1898, more than 30,000 troops were dispatched to Tampa. In contrast to the luxurious accommodations of the Tampa Bay Hotel, the regiments of Army regulars and volunteers pitched their tents in the dusty sand surrounding Tampa. Army-issued tents consisted of canvas supported by a wood frame. (TRC.)

This group of men is identified as part of the 1st US Volunteer Cavalry Regiment, nicknamed the Rough Riders. Formed to fight during the Spanish-American War, they were composed of Western cowboys, Native Americans, and East Coast polo players, under the command of Col. Leonard Wood. Assistant Secretary of the Navy Theodore Roosevelt resigned his position to join the elite group as a lieutenant colonel. More than 1,000 Rough Riders came to Tampa. (HD.)

Clara Barton, founder of the American Red Cross, came to Tampa on April 27, 1898, to oversee the Red Cross efforts in preparation for the invasion of Cuba. Scores of Red Cross nurses followed to care for the soldiers. Barton is in the center of the image, easily identified by her dark dress. (ARC.)

Correspondents and foreign attachés pose under the palms on the hotel grounds. By one account, 128 press passes were distributed to correspondents in Tampa. Among them were Stephen Crane (in the white suit) and Richard Harding Davis (wearing the helmet). At the age of 25, Crane set out to cover the Spanish-American War in Cuba as a journalist for several newspapers, including William Randolph Hearst's *New York Journal*. (TRC.)

Gen. Fitzhugh Lee, a Confederate cavalry officer during the Civil War and the nephew of Robert E. Lee, attended a council of war at the Tampa Bay Hotel. This image was viewed with a magic lantern, a projector for showing glass slides. The photograph was taken by Dwight L. Elmendorf, a painter who became a photographer known for his hand-colored lantern slides and popular lectures. (TRC.)

During April and May 1898, the press and the officers enjoyed the luxury of the Tampa Bay Hotel, which inspired the phrase "The Rocking Chair War." Here, from left to right, Maj. Gen. James F. Wade, Samuel Ramsey of *McClure's Magazine*, and First Lieutenant Ramsey are seated on the hotel's west veranda. (TRC.)

This sentinel was photographed at a camp in Tampa holding his rifle with fixed bayonet. The soldiers' uniforms were government-issued dark-blue wool jackets and light-blue wool pants, which contrasted with the Rough Riders' cotton khaki uniforms.

This stereo card of an encampment shows a close-up of camp life in Tampa. In this rare image, a lady is visiting the soldiers, with a group of civilians in the background. The museum's archives contain numerous stereoscopic views of the Spanish-American War.

While the officers rocked in their chairs on the veranda at the hotel and traded stories with the correspondents, the enlisted and volunteer troops drilled under the hot sun. It would have been easy for these young men to let down their guard while they waited for two months to deploy, but their days were filled with drills. This view shows the 25th Infantry firing from breastworks while in Tampa.

The 9th and 10th Cavalry Regiments were the African American units, known as the Buffalo Soldiers. Artist Frederic Remington made this sketch of the 9th Cavalry riding through the pines at Port Tampa. The 9th and 10th Regiments were instrumental in the success of the Battle of San Juan Hill.

This stereoscopic view is entitled "Pay-Day, US Army, Camp Tampa, Florida, U.S.A." Army privates were paid $13 per month. In Tampa, rations were scarce. Payday made it possible for the men to buy additional food or entertainment in town. This card was produced by Underwood & Underwood, one of the most prominent stereo card companies in the United States during the 1880s and 1890s.

A Cavalry Camp, Tampa, Fla.
Copyright 1898 by R. Y. Young.

Stereo cards were popular among middle-class families during the late 19th century. Viewing them was a common pastime. People collected images of tourist sites they had visited, exotic destinations they would only experience through the stereoscope, news events, and mini-stories. Sketch artists captured the energy of battle, but stereoscopic views provided a detailed look at the everyday aspects of the military campaign. People could purchase stereo cards by mail order, from door-to-door salesmen, or in stores, individually or as boxed sets.

As they waited for orders to ship out, troops filled their days with drills and preparation for combat, but they also found time for leisure activities. A raucous splash in the water was welcome relief from the sweltering heat. This stereo card's caption reads, "Soldier Boys' Recreation, Tampa, Florida."

The caption for this stereo card reads, "Dearest Annie, To-morrow we move on toward Santiago where we expect a hard battle." Many of the men used their leisure time to maintain a connection with loved ones. The Tampa postmaster was inundated with the high volume of letters moving through the small post office. He received hundreds of requests to forward mail as the troops moved from camp to camp.

This view is titled "The Barber Shop of the Soldiers' Camp, Tampa Florida, U.S.A." President McKinley requested 125,000 volunteers to join the effort. Even though they were far from home and without many of the amenities to which they were accustomed, basic necessities could be found in camp.

This view shows "Bouncing a New Recruit," an activity that was good sport and a good team-building exercise. The men used one of their Army-issued blankets to toss a new recruit into the air and catch him as he came down.

Attachés from around the world traveled to Tampa to observe the military operation. The British attaché Capt. Arthur H. Lee (left), stands by the main entrance to the hotel on the east veranda with Count von Goetzen (right), Germany's military attaché. The skylights embedded in the wooden floor that illuminated the basement below are visible from this perspective. (TRC.)

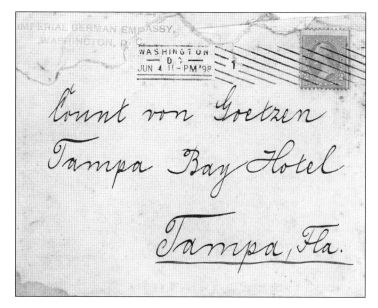

This envelope is addressed to Count von Goetzen at the Tampa Bay Hotel. It was sent from the Imperial German Embassy in Washington, DC, and postmarked June 4, 1898, at 11:00 p.m. Count von Goetzen was a personal friend of the Kaiser. After the Spanish-American War, von Goetzen foretold that Germany would start a great war in 15 years. His prediction of World War I was off by only one year.

Officers' wives were among the civilians who came to Tampa during the waiting period. Everyone gathered in the hotel for the nightly concert by one of the regimental bands. On April 27, 1898, the *New York Times* reported that Henry and Margaret Plant "will give an elaborate reception and ball in honor of General Wade and the other officers. This affair is expected to break the ice, and begin a gay, though limited, military season." According to Richard Harding Davis, one young officer compared the dances "to a ball at Brussels on the night before Waterloo."

"Waiting to Go To Cuba: Dance and Reception Given to the American Officers at Tampa Bay Hotel. The Spanish-American War: With the United States Army at Tampa" is a lithograph published June 11, 1898, in the *Graphic*. This sketch by Douglas Macpherson shows officers and guests in the hotel lobby. This view was later reproduced as a colorized stereo card titled "Reception to Officers at Tampa Bay Hotel."

As the waiting dragged on, life at the Tampa Bay Hotel became a social experience. The hotel was open to the general public, who used the opportunity to meet notable generals and members of the press. Some civilian guests collected autographs from the press. Douglas Macpherson, sketch artist for the *Graphic*, a British weekly illustrated newspaper, was one of the reporters who signed his name in this autograph album.

"American Officers awaiting embarkation for Cuba at Tampa Bay Hotel Celebrating the Queen's Birthday," a sketch by Douglas Macpherson, appeared in the *Graphic* on June 18, 1898. It documents a celebratory moment in the dining room of officers toasting Queen Victoria's birthday and the ties of friendship between the United States and Great Britain. As reported in numerous newspapers across the country, both General Shafter and Plant offered remarks at the event.

British attaché Arthur H. Lee (standing at far right) and Count von Goetzen (in white suit) are pictured with representatives from Austria, Japan, and Great Britain on a bench in the hotel garden. While many of the press and diplomatic dignitaries stayed at the hotel, some newspapers reported that a few of the correspondents opted to sleep in tents with the soldiers when the hotel rates reached $6 per night.

Pictured on the steps of the Tampa Bay Casino are Maj. Gen. James F. Wade and his staff. From left to right are Lt. Col. Arthur McArthur, adjunct general for the Corps; Major General Wade; Lieutenants W.E. Almy and G.W. Reed of the US 1st Cavalry; Maj. D.D. Wheeler, chief quartermaster; and First Lieutenant Ramsey. Wade was commanding officer of troops in Tampa until Generals Miles and Shafter arrived.

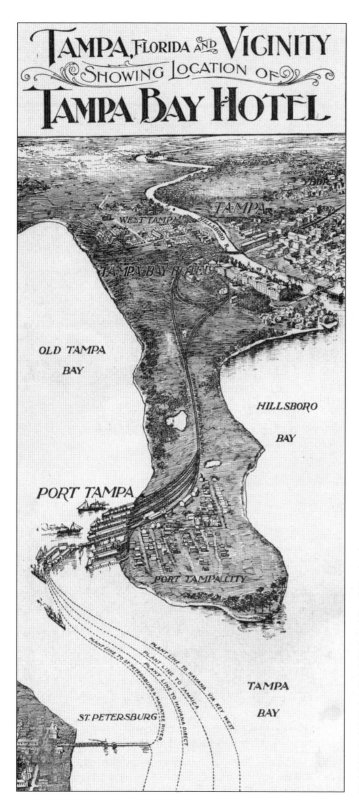

This 1898 map illustrates the location of Port Tampa, nine miles south of the US Army headquarters at the Tampa Bay Hotel. The two points were connected by the Plant System's single rail line. Four of the steamship lines to Cuba are also identified. Plant's steamships the SS *Florida*, *Olivette*, and *Mascotte*, in addition to 38 other vessels, participated in the Cuban Campaign. Each of Plant's ships could transport three regiments.

When the Army began to mobilize, Port Tampa became a crowded, chaotic, noisy, dusty mess. Under the sweltering sun, troops waited to board ships, stevedores carried equipment from the trains to the steamers, supplies piled up, and animals added to the confusion. This stereo card captures the bustle of activity and bears the caption "Dock at Tampa on the Day of Sailing for Santiago de Cuba."

This stereoscopic view shows the port and the flurry of activity surrounding the process of transferring cargo from train cars to ships for embarkation to Cuba. American troops with their gear amassed near the railroad track at Port Tampa wait to board the ships.

Army troops load supplies aboard a Plant System ship. The company logo—a "P" in a cross formée—is visible on the smokestack. The Port Tampa channel could accommodate three rows of eight ships lined up bow to stern. The cargo was loaded across the first line of ships to the second line. Plant's *Olivette* was designated as a hospital ship and as transport for the hospital corps and press, according to the *New York Times* of June 15, 1898.

The mules for the Cuban invasion are being loaded onto steamships docked at Port Tampa. The commanding officers received orders to load the troops on June 8. After everything was on board, Washington sent a second order to wait. Inaccurate reports indicated that Spanish ships were in the area. For four days, US troops waited aboard the ships before finally sailing out of Port Tampa on June 14.

This unique perspective shows a long view of Port Tampa from atop a railcar running along the single track leading into the port. The Inn at Port Tampa, another Plant System hotel, is visible on the right. Clara Barton and a number of Red Cross nurses stayed at the inn during the planning stage of the Cuban Campaign.

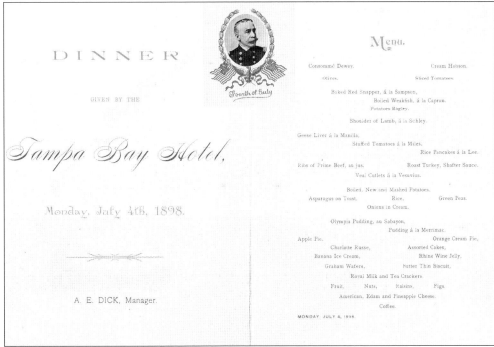

The hotel chef created a special menu for July 4, 1898, honoring those who had served with distinction. Special dishes included Consommé Dewey, Stuffed Tomatoes á la Miles, Rice Pancakes á la Lee, Roast Turkey with Shafter Sauce, and Pudding á la Merrimac. The Spanish forces in Cuba surrendered on July 17, 1898. The hotel closed as Army headquarters on July 21, 1898, to prepare for the new tourist season in November.

BIBLIOGRAPHY

Braden, Susan R. *The Architecture of Leisure: The Florida Resort Hotels of Henry Flagler and Henry Plant*. Gainesville, FL: University Press of Florida, 2002.

Browning, Alex. *Tampa Bay Hotel Co.* Unpublished memoir, 1933.

Brundage, W. Fitzhugh. *The Southern Past: A Clash of Race and Memory*. Cambridge, MA: Belknap Press, 2005.

Covington, James W. "The Tampa Bay Hotel." *Tequesta* 26 (1966): 3–20.

Davis, Richard Harding. *The Cuban and Porto Rican Campaigns*. New York, NY: Charles Scribner's Sons, 1898.

Drysdale, William. "Even 'Front' May Get Lost." *New York Times*. February 8, 1891.

——— "Florida's January Suns." *New York Times*. January 31, 1892.

——— "The Shores Of Tampa Bay." *New York Times*. January 24, 1892.

"Fiehe Plans New Gardens." *Tampa Tribune*. July 14, 1901.

Hall, Valentine G., ed. *Wright & Ditson's Lawn Tennis Guide for 1892*. Boston, MA: Wright & Ditson, 1992.

Hewitt, Nancy A. *Southern Discomfort: Women's Activism in Tampa, Florida, 1880s–1920s*. Urbana, IL: University of Illinois Press, 2001.

Knetsch, Joe and Nick Wynne. *Florida in the Spanish-American War*. Charleston, SC: History Press, 2011.

Roberts, Larry. *Florida's Golden Age of Souvenirs, 1890–1930*. Gainesville, FL: University Press of Florida, 2001.

Sandoval-Strausz, A.K. *Hotel: An American History*. New Haven, CT: Yale University Press, 2007.

"Tis Done!" *Tampa Daily Journal*. February 6, 1891.

ABOUT THE ORGANIZATION

The Henry B. Plant Museum is a museum to one of the finest hotels ever built. Unlike most museums dedicated to lifestyles of the past, it contains the actual furnishings enjoyed by the first guests to visit. The museum accurately reflects the opulence of turn-of-the-century America and the vision of transportation pioneer Henry B. Plant, who opened the Tampa Bay Hotel in 1891. Today, the museum occupies a portion of the old hotel; the distinguished University of Tampa, the remainder. The Moorish Revival architecture and original furnishings have made the former hotel one of the Tampa Bay area's greatest sources of pride, earning distinction as a National Historic Landmark.

After the hotel closed in 1932, the museum was created by mayoral decree in 1933 and became Tampa's first museum. The museum interprets the Tampa Bay Hotel and the Victorian lifestyles of America's Gilded Age for people of all ages, backgrounds, and levels of interest. The museum transports the visitor, through educational exhibits and events, to the late Victorian period, the beginning of Florida's tourism industry, and the early years of the City of Tampa.

Electric lighting was rare in the 19th century, but the very modern Tampa Bay Hotel was grandly illuminated. Today, the museum recreates the original lighting of the hotel with reproduction Edison carbon filament bulbs. What seems to be very dim today was described as "ablaze" in 1891.

The museum staff is committed to providing outstanding service to guests and making their experience memorable, offering a gracious welcome to everyone who walks through the door, assuring a friendly and helpful atmosphere to all.

Henry B. Plant Museum
401 West Kennedy Boulevard
Tampa, FL 33606
813-254-1891
plantmuseum.com

Discover Thousands of Local History Books Featuring Millions of Vintage Images

Arcadia Publishing, the leading local history publisher in the United States, is committed to making history accessible and meaningful through publishing books that celebrate and preserve the heritage of America's people and places.

Find more books like this at
www.arcadiapublishing.com

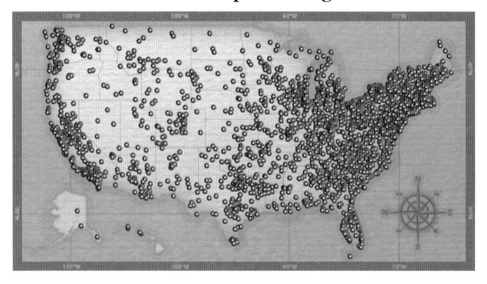

Search for your hometown history, your old stomping grounds, and even your favorite sports team.